BLOODLINE
OF THE
GODS

BLOODLINE

OF THE

GODS

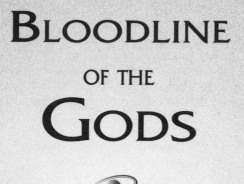

Unravel the Mystery of the Human Blood Type

to Reveal the Aliens Among Us

By

Nick Redfern

NEW PAGE BOOKS
A division of The Career Press, Inc.
Wayne, NJ

BLOODLINE OF THE GODS
EDITED BY JODI BRANDON
TYPESET BY EILEEN MUNSON
Cover illustration by noir33
Printed in the U.S.A.

To order this title, please call toll-free 1-800-CAREER-1 (NJ and Canada: 201-848-0310) to order using VISA or MasterCard, or for further information on books from Career Press.

The Career Press, Inc.
12 Parish Drive,
Wayne, NJ
www.careerpress.com
www.newpagebooks.com

Library of Congress Cataloging-in-Publication Data
Redfern, Nicholas, 1964-
  Bloodline of the gods : unravel the mystery in human blood to reveal the aliens among us / by Nick Redfern.
      pages cm
  Includes bibliographical references and index.
  ISBN 978-1-60163-365-1 -- ISBN 978-1-60163-387-3 (ebook) 1. Human-alien encounters--History. 2. Rh factor--Miscellanea. 3. Civilization, Ancient--Extraterrestrial influences. I. Title.

  BF2050.R4345 2014
  001.942--dc23

                      2015010672

Image Credits

Image on page 17 courtesy of Wikimedia Commons.

Image on page 26, F. Éditeur Sinnet, 1852. Courtesy of Wikimedia Commons.

Image on page 37, Viktor M. Vasnetsov, 1883. Courtesy of Wikimedia Commons.

Image on page 46, Hermann Schaaffhausen, 1888. Courtesy of Wikimedia Commons.

Image on page 55, P. de Hondt, 1728. Courtesy of Wikimedia Commons.

Image on page 66, George Frederic Watts, 1885. Courtesy of Wikimedia Commons.

Image on page 85, John Martin, 1852. Courtesy of Wikimedia Commons.

Image on page 92, John Collier, 1892. Courtesy of Wikimedia Commons.

Image on page 108, Henry Fuseli, 1781. Courtesy of Wikimedia Commons.

Image on page 115, John Bauer, 1910. Courtesy of Wikimedia Commons.

Image on page 121, Central Intelligence Agency, 2015. Courtesy of Wikimedia Commons.

Image on page 134, Emery Walker, 1908. Courtesy of Wikimedia Commons.

Image on page 141, U.S. government, 2005. Courtesy of Wikimedia Commons.

Image on pages 147, 178, and 213, 16th century, source unknown. Courtesy of Wikimedia Commons.

Image on page 152, copyright 2000. Courtesy of the author.

Image on page 163, copyright 2005. Courtesy of the author.

Image on page 170, Martino di Bartolomeo, 15th century. Courtesy of Wikimedia Commons.

Image on page 186, U.S. government, 2013. Courtesy of Wikimedia Commons.

Image on page 206, U.S. government, 1963. Courtesy of Wikimedia Commons.

Image on page 223, Tiiu Sild, 1967. Courtesy of Wikimedia Commons.

· Acknowledgments ·

I would like to offer my very sincere thanks and deep appreciation to everyone at New Page Books and Career Press, particularly Michael Pye, Laurie Kelly-Pye, Kirsten Dalley, Jeff Piasky, and Adam Schwartz; and to all the staff at Warwick Associates for their fine promotion and publicity campaigns. I would also like to say a very big thank you to my literary agent, Lisa Hagan, for all her tireless hard work, help, and enthusiasm.

· Contents ·

· Introduction ·

The story you are about to read is, by my own admission, controversial in the extreme, and for a number of reasons. It is a story that requires us to accept the possibility that the history of the human race is woefully incomplete, incorrect, and lacking in key, critical data. It is also a story that suggests humankind, as we know it, and as we are taught, is not exactly what it appears to be, and never has been. Put simply, a small percentage of humanity—around 10 to 15 percent—is different from the rest. And not just slightly different, but *incredibly* different: physically, mentally, spiritually, and, even, psychically different. This near-unique body of individuals are the Rh negatives, a term taken from the fact that their blood is, in a word, unique. Its very existence goes against everything that Charles Darwin stood for, and that Darwinism and the Theory of Evolution *still* stand for, today.

Perhaps most controversial of all, the story that *Bloodline of the Gods* tells demands that we take a very close look at our gods—or God, depending upon one's own, particular belief system—and see them for what they may really have been, and still may be: not all-powerful, supernatural deities; nor the creators of all things; and not entities that decide our fates in a hellish or heavenly afterlife. The story presents our gods as something acutely different, to the point that some will, no doubt, consider what follows to be nothing less than downright heresy.

Our gods may well, in reality, have been nothing of the sort. They may have been a race of incredibly ancient, and fantastically long-lived, extraterrestrials—creatures from a world far away and who came to the Earth, on an emergency mission, when both their own civilization and their home planet were looking extinction, and the end of all things, firmly in the eye. In an effort to save their species, they effectively wildly turned the Earth on its head and into one big factory—mining the entire planet for precious materials, and using highly advanced technologies to genetically mutate and upgrade a certain, early humanoid: *Homo erectus*. It's a story that takes us from the millennia-old plains of Africa to the people of ancient Sumer and Babylonia, and from the early people of Europe to select souls of today, who appear to be the helpless victims in a program of alien-driven, inter-species experimentation.

What was once a primitive human, one that—had the "gods" not chosen to intervene—might very well have retained its proto-form forever, was radically transformed into something else: a new breed of creature, one that was destined to toil for ancient astronauts as a downtrodden, submissive slave race. It literally was a case of injecting new blood into the early human species, as a means to control it and exploit it. And out of all this species-manipulating were born the Rh negatives.

In the hundreds of thousands of years that have passed since the human race became nothing but a planet-wide laboratory experiment for cruel, self-absorbed extraterrestrials, the aliens have certainly left their mark—even if most people don't realize it or endorse it. Most noticeably so on Cro-Magnon man of yesteryear, and on the Basque people of Spain and France, too—all of who can accurately be said to be the genetic offspring of the gods. Those planet-hopping entities have also left their distinct mark on what have become known as "alien abductees," people in the modern era who—just like *Homo erectus* in the distant past—have been subjected to distressing experiments, tests, procedures, and probing of a genetic, reproductive nature. What was undertaken in a wide open situation hundreds of thousands of years ago still continues today, albeit in deep, unsettling stealth.

All of this brings us to a number of critical questions that will both be addressed and answered in the pages that follow. Who *really* were the gods? What was the nature of the critical emergency that prompted them to take complete and utter control of the Earth, hundreds of thousands of years ago—to mutate an early form of humanoid, and, ultimately, in the process, become the foundation of some of the world's major and most cherished religions?

There are other important questions that need to be answered, too. Do today's Rh negatives—those born out of nothing less than an archaic, alien bloodline—pose a threat to the rest of society? Or are they just about as much in the dark on the matter of their incredible origins as most people are? In what ways, mentally and physically, are they different from the rest of us? Why do so many Rh negatives hold positions of power, in both government and royalty? And why have they done so for eons? Are extraterrestrials creating growing numbers of Rh negatives for sinister purposes—ones that may revolve around the establishment of an underground army, a combined "Trojan Horse," the purpose of which has at its heart the manipulation and control of human civilization? Are alien-human "hybrids" of an Rh nature engaged in nefarious, worldwide activities? Could we, one day, see a violent backlash against the Rh negatives, if proof of their astonishing, alien origins is forthcoming? Will human civilization become splintered and split into an "us and them" situation and mentality?

The questions are many. The answers are amazing. Whether those questions and answers are what people wish to hear, however, is a very different matter. Billions of people hold their beloved religious beliefs close to their hearts. And they don't want to be told anything that might cast doubt on those same beliefs. To what extent they *should* embrace them, however—*even if at all*, given that the gods may be nothing more than someone else's equivalent of NASA's Apollo astronauts—is an issue that gets to the very heart of this story.

Bloodline of the Gods is not anti-religion. Nor is its agenda to undermine religion. Rather, it simply offers the reader an alternative viewpoint on the origins of the human race, of what we are, of how we came to be, and why—in terms of the Rh negatives—a sizeable percentage of the world's population is something other than it seems to be.

· The Nature of the Negatives ·

To fully appreciate the profoundly weird nature of this potentially otherworldly saga, it's most important to first demonstrate how radically different those with Rh negative blood are to the remainder of the world's population. We will then tackle the critical matter of why the Rh negatives even exist at all. For the human race, there are four, primary, types of blood: A, B, AB, and O. The classifications are derived from the antigens of a person's blood cells—antigens being proteins that are found on the surface of the cells and that are designed to combat bacteria and viruses. Most of the human population has such proteins on their cells. They are the Rh positive percentage of the Earth's people. Within the United States, current estimates suggest that around 85 percent of all Caucasians, roughly 90 percent of African Americans, and approximately 98 percent of Asian Americans are Rh positive.

The small percentage of the U.S. population (and that of the rest of the world, too, it should be noted) that does not exhibit the relevant proteins falls into a very different category—that of the Rh negatives. There is, however, another, third group of people, the Basques of central Spain and the western parts of France, whose percentage of RH negatives is incredibly high: close to an amazing 40 percent.

On top of that, and at the opposite end of the spectrum, the Basques almost completely lack individuals with B and AB blood. Why one particular group of people should be so incredibly different from just about everyone else, is a matter that will be discussed and dissected in the next chapter of this book.

The Nature of Blood

It was not until the dawning of the 20th century that the first, initial steps were taken to fully understand the precise nature of blood. As incredible as it may sound, however, experiments to transfuse blood from human to human, and from animal to animal, date back as far as the mid-1600s, when experiments using dogs and sheep proved to be successful—at least, to a degree they were successful. Despite the ups and downs of these early experiments, right up until the latter part of the 19th century, matters were very much misunderstood on the issue of blood—and, very often, tragically so, too. This all became acutely clear during the turbulent American Civil War of 1861 to 1865, in which no less than 600,000 individuals lost their lives, as North and South went to war in violent and bloody fashion.

When trying to save the lives of soldiers exhibiting terrible, battlefield-based wounds from the devastating effects of bullets, blades, and cannons—many of which provoked significant and life-threatening blood loss—military doctors were left with no option but to transfuse blood from healthy and hardy individuals into the bloodstreams of the critically injured. On some occasions, the procedures worked perfectly. On other occasions, however, they had the exact opposite outcome: The patients soon died. The reason for this distinct Russian roulette–style situation was a deep mystery, at the time. As a result, transfusions in the United States were seen as being very much a last resort; in much of Europe of the 1800s, however, blood transfusions were viewed not as a last resort, but as a definitive no-go area—period.

At least, that is where things stood until the first decade of the 20th century. That is when history was well and truly made by a man named Karl Landsteiner, a Nobel Prize–winning physician and biologist from Austria, a man who forever changed the face of medicine, and who also happened to be the co-discoverer (with Romanian microbiologist Constantin Levaditi and Erwin Popper, an Austrian physician) of the polio virus.

The Matter of the Rhesus Macaque

Karl Landsteiner's groundbreaking work demonstrated something that, at the time, was deemed remarkable: Blood serum (the liquid portion that encompasses the blood cells of the human body) is not identical in all individuals. Landsteiner's studies revealed that there was not just one blood group, after all. Four decades later, Landsteiner and a colleague, a New York Doctor of Medicine named Alexander Solomon Weiner, stumbled upon something else—something equally as remarkable as Landsteiner's earlier discoveries. As well as conducting groundbreaking research in relation to matters concerning human blood and their various groups, Landsteiner and Weiner undertook experimentation on monkeys, specifically on Rhesus macaques.

They are what are termed "Old World Monkeys" and can be found across much of south and central Asia,

Physician and biologist Karl Landsteiner, 1930.

their territory extending from Afghanistan to China. Not only that, Rhesus macaques and the human race shared a common ancestor up until around 25 million years ago, when a divergence occurred and the two went their separate ways. On top of that, macaques have a DNA sequence that is 93-percent identical to that of the human race. This latter issue of a close tie between Rhesus macaques and people is why so much research into human diseases and viruses is under-taken on macaques.

Murray B. Gardner and Paul A. Luciw, in "Macaque Models of Human Infectious Disease," say on this particular issue:

> Macaques have served as models for more than 70 human infectious diseases of diverse etiologies, including a multi-tude of agents—bacteria, viruses, fungi, parasites, prions. The remarkable diversity of human infectious diseases that have been modeled in the macaque includes global, childhood, and tropical diseases as well as newly emergent, sexually transmitted, oncogenic, degenerative neurologic, potential bioterrorism, and miscellaneous other diseases (Gardner & Luciw, 2008).

Landsteiner and Weiner, during the course of their stud-ies, elected to inject the blood of the Rhesus macaques into other, very different animals, including both guinea pigs and rabbits. It was an action that caused the blood of the animals to clot. To his astonishment, Landsteiner found that the clotting was caused by a further antigen, or protein, that, up until 1940, had not been recog-nized or even detected by anyone in the medical community. Most significant of all, additional work demonstrated that the hitherto-unknown antigen at issue was also found to be present in people. Landsteiner decided to term it the "Rh factor" ("Rh" standing for "Rhesus," of course). And there was yet another discovery too, one that gets to the very heart of the subject matter of this book: that there were some individuals who completely lacked the Rh factor (a rarity in the overall 33 types of human blood). They were, and are, the Rh negatives. There were more than a few of them, too. And, as history has shown, and as will later be demonstrated, the negatives amount to a group of people filled with anomalies that place them in a category noticeably detached and different from the rest of the populace.

When a Mother Attempts to Kill Her Baby

The most significant—and also deeply worrying—side effect of being Rh negative relates to the matter of pregnancy. Actually, it's the one and only adverse side effect: Giving birth aside, being Rh negative has no major, adverse bearing whatsoever upon matters relative to health. In fact, and as will become clearer in a later chapter, there may very well be notable benefits, health-wise, when it comes to being Rh negative. For a pregnant woman who is Rh negative, however, the hazards can be both considerable and extremely dangerous. If a woman who is Rh negative is made pregnant by a man who is also Rh negative, the problems are non-existent and there is no need for concern: Both individuals are wholly compatible with one another, the fetus will develop in normal fashion, and the child will be born Rh negative. If, however, the father is Rh positive and the mother is Rh negative, problems can begin and the results may prove to be very different—and tragically so, too, as the developing fetus will be Rh positive. It is this latter issue that gets to the very crux of the problem.

As incredible as it may sound, the blood of an Rh negative pregnant woman can be completely incompatible with the blood of an Rh positive baby that she is carrying. Such a situation can very often provoke the mother's own blood to produce potentially lethal antibodies, which are designed to attack the fetus's blood, if and when the former is exposed to the latter. In other words, the Rh positive baby is perceived by the mother's negative immune system as something hostile. For all intents and purposes, the unborn child is considered something *alien* and something to be gotten rid of at the earliest opportunity possible.

The process by which the mother effectively tries to attack and kill its very own offspring via the blood is termed sensitization. In this peculiar process, the mother's blood crosses into the placenta and then into what is termed the fetal circulation, where it proceeds to wage war on the baby's blood cells, which are made in the bone marrow, and which are absolutely vital for the carrying of oxygen about the body. It's a war to the death, for all intents and purposes.

Systematically, and bit by bit, the mother's antibodies attack the red blood cells of the baby, breaking them down and provoking the development of what is termed hemolytic anemia. And when hemolytic anemia begins to overwhelm the fetus, the results can be disastrous and deadly. Anemia in an adult can be a serious issue; in an unborn child it can be even more so. Organs, particularly so the heart, can be significantly and irreversibly damaged. The lack of sufficient levels of oxygen may have a disastrous effect on the development and function of the brain. In a worst-case scenario, the fetus may die.

More disturbing is the fact that the more times a woman becomes pregnant, the more powerful and prevalent the deadly antibodies become. In short, the mother's body finds ways to make the process of trying to kill the fetus ever more powerful, swift, and effective with each successive pregnancy. It's almost as if there is something deeply *ancient and alien* encoded in our DNA that sees positive and negative as being acutely different to one another, and never intended for unification. Later on, we will see why that may be *exactly* the case.

Fortunately for a pregnant negative, there are ways and means to combat the mother's violent assault on her unborn child. Rh immune globulin is a blood product that is injected (via a muscle) into the mother and that prevents her body from developing the very type of antibodies that are designed to attack the fetus—providing, that is, she is not already sensitized to the Rh factor. If she isn't, the chances are extremely high that the pregnancy will proceed in regular fashion and the fetus will develop into a normal, healthy baby.

There is another anomaly with Rh negative blood—although this one is of a positive nature. I mentioned earlier that there are four primary types of blood: A, B, AB, and O. These types apply both to people who are Rh positive and those who are Rh negative. It transpires that Type O negative is rather unique, in the sense that it can be successfully transfused into just about anyone and everyone—regardless of their personal blood group and without causing fatal, or even adverse, reactions. For this particular reason emergency response teams very often carry Type O negative blood when responding to disasters; it's pretty much guaranteed to be acceptable to anyone needing blood in a life-or-death situation. On the other hand, however, those with O negative blood can only be transfused with O negative blood; for them, nothing else will work. Among the negatives, then, the Type O variety appears to be the most unique of all. A case of keeping the bloodline completely pure, perhaps. And, maybe, a deliberately engineered, case, too.

Before we get to the controversial matter of ancient extraterrestrials manipulating the human bloodline in the distant past, it's important that we first rule out down-to-earth explanations for the Rh negative factor. After all, asserting that some of us are the product of alien gene-tinkering is not something that should be done lightly. Keeping that in mind, is it feasible that the controversy could be due to nothing stranger than natural selection or mutation of a very down-to-earth variety? Such a scenario might, at first glance, seem wholly reasonable. After all, some of us have dark skin, and others have light skin. One person has blond hair, another has black, and a third has brown. Eye color can vary wildly too: The pigmentation of the iris ranges from blue to green, and gray to brown. Very occasionally, a person will be born with amber-colored eyes, or even with eyes of different colors.

The color variations in skin, hair, and eyes are chiefly caused by nothing stranger than a pigment called melanin. So, in that sense, it's not impossible that the Rh negative factor is one that could have developed naturally, rather than as a result of the intervention of fantastic, extraterrestrial technologies. There are, however, certain issues that suggest Mother Nature was not the responsible party. It's very important to note there is no evidence to suggest that the color of skin, hair, or eyes can have a bearing upon the personality, mindset, or belief systems of an individual. Blood of one particular type, however, can have such a bearing—and a highly significant one, too, in certain people.

Those with Rh negative blood are very often of a specific mindset, displaying a deep and keen interest in science, UFOs, and unexplained phenomena. They have higher-than-average psychic abilities, such as precognition and extrasensory perception. Their IQ is typically higher than that of most people. Physically, they are different too: A low body temperature, slow pulse, extra vertebrae, and low blood pressure are all common in the Rh negatives. They are far more resilient to illness, viruses, and disease than the rest of the human population. And, as we will see later, there is good evidence in hand that demonstrates clandestine groups within both the U.S. government and military have secretly monitored the rise of the Rh negatives and carefully studied their associations to the UFO phenomenon.

When we put all of this together, we are faced with what appears to be nothing less than a careful, controlled, manipulation of certain portions of the human race, both physically and mentally. Can we prove that nature was not the overriding factor in the Rh negative controversy? No. Can we make a very strong case that an outside force—one that had its origins on another world—was the party responsible for creating a unique, improved form of human? Most certainly, as you will now see.

With all of the above now said, it's time to take a look at the one group of people who—more than any other, anywhere on the planet—can accurately be termed the reigning negatives. They are the Basque people of Spain and France. Their story is a long and winding one—a story that may very well have at its heart, and at its origins, evidence of genetic manipulation of the human race in the distant past by none other than powerful and infinitely advanced extraterrestrials. In our efforts to understand the negatives of today—as well as a potential ongoing and secret alien agenda, of a genetics-based nature, in our very midst—a trip into the distant and turbulent past is now in order.

· The Blood of the Basques ·

In *Atlantis: The Antediluvian World*, Ignatius Donnelly described the Basques as

> of middle size, compactly built, robust and agile, of a darker complexion than the Spaniards, with gray eyes and black hair. They are simple but proud, impetuous, merry, and hospitable. The women are beautiful, skillful in performing men's work, and remarkable for their vivacity and grace. The Basques are much attached to dancing, and are very fond of the music of the bagpipe (Donnelly, 2010).

There is more to the Basques than that, however—*far* more. The story of the Basque people is as mind-bending as it is almost unique. It's also a story steeped in fog-shrouded mystery and intrigue. Not only that, the implications of the story are stunning: The Basques just might be the results of highly advanced genetic manipulation by visiting extraterrestrials (ETs) untold number of millennia ago. If such a scenario sounds incredible, well, that's exactly what it is. In a situation like this, there's only one place to start: the beginning.

The Basques: a Unique People

The Basques take their name from the area in which they live today: the Basque Country. It's located in the western portion of the vast and icy Pyrenees Mountains, which border Spain and France and which run for in excess of 300 miles. Presently, the area is home to more than two million people and is dominated by the cities of San Sebastian and Bilbao. The Basques—"Basque" meaning "population," "land," and "nation," among a number of additional terms—are an ancient people who were known to both the Greeks and the Romans. Chronicling the early history of the Basques is no easy task, as the people of that era left not even a single written word whatsoever pertaining to their culture, their lives, and their beliefs and traditions. We do, however, know that the Middle Ages was a turbulent time for the Basques, as near-endless turf wars with opposing lands and armies occupied much of their time. Today, many Basques proudly consider themselves a people distinct and different from their fellow Spanish and French. They have very good reason, too.

The Basques: the world's most famous Rh negatives.

The Origins of the Basques

The specific period in which the Basques first began to flourish is a matter of deep debate. One school of thought suggests that the Basques are the last surviving remnants of what was Paleolithic man. The Paleolithic period extended from more than 2.6 million BC to around 10,000 BC. At some point in this extensive time frame, early humans—proto-Basques, one might be justified in calling them—surfaced and thrived, eventually becoming the Basque people as we know them today. In addition, archaeological remains demonstrate the presence of a culture in the Basque country during the time of the Aurignacian culture, which ran from approximately 45,000 to 35,000 years ago. Indeed, Cro-Magnon man (an integral part of this story and who will be discussed in future chapters) moved into that very area during the final stages of this period, firmly elbowing out of the picture the ultimately doomed Neanderthals.

Another theory suggests that the Basques are an outgrowth of the people of an area covering parts of southern France and northern Spain called the Franco-Cantabrian region. It so happens that it's a region in which some of the finest of all cave murals of the Paleolithic period can be found. Certainly, the most famous and highly regarded murals are located within the Lascaux caves, situated close to Dordogne, France, and date back to more than 17,000 years ago. The artwork—primarily of animals and more than 2,000 in number—is, to put it bluntly, stunning, and blows away any and all images of savage, dumb, club-wielding "cave men."

There is, however, a distinct possibility that although the Basques certainly had a major presence in the Franco-Cantabrian region, it may not have been their original point of origin. Studies undertaken by linguists suggest a potential linkage between the Basque language and that of the ancient people of North Africa. Stephen Oppenheimer, in *The Origins of the British*, suggests that it may have been about 16,000 BC—when temperatures were still warm and the next Ice Age was still a considerable number of centuries away—that the original Basques made their trek from Africa to Europe. They very likely brought with them their language, too, one that has no less than seven dialects. And on the matter of that language...

A Unique and Ancient Tongue

Adding much weight to the notable nature of the Basques is the fact that their native tongue, which is known as Euskara, is wholly unique across Europe. In fact, it's unique to *the entire planet.* In his three-volume series *The History of Rome* (which was written between 1838 and 1842 and remained unfinished, due to the author's death in 1842) Thomas Arnold said of the language of the Basque people:

> ...its unlikeness to the other languages of Europe is very striking, even when compared with Welsh, or with Sclavonic. The affinities of the Welsh numerals with those of the Teutonic languages, and the Greek and Latin, are obvious at the first glance; and the same may be said of most of the Sclavonic numerals; but the Basque are so peculiar, that it is difficult to identify any one of them, except "sei" "six," with those of other languages (Arnold, 2006).

Arnold could only state one thing with certainty when it came to the curious language of the Basques: It showed evidence of "great antiquity." Clearly, there is a fog-shrouded history to the Basques that remains tantalizingly incomplete. It's something we will return to, in due course and as our story develops (Ibid.).

In 1877, Wentworth Webster, in *Basque Legends*, came straight to the point when he noted: "At present, no language has been discovered which presents any root-likeness to the Basque, analogous to that which exists." That situation remains pretty much identical today (Webster, 1877).

Five years later, in his classic title of the mysteries of the distant past, *Atlantis: The Antediluvian World*, Ignatius Donnelly quoted linguist Peter Stephen Du Ponceau as saying:

> This language, preserved in a corner of Europe by a few thousand mountaineers, is the sole remaining fragment of,

perhaps, a hundred dialects constructed on the same plan, which probably existed and were universally spoken at a remote period in that quarter of the world. Like the bones of the mammoth, it remains a monument of the destruction produced by a succession of ages. It stands single and alone of its kind, surrounded by idioms that have no affinity with it (Donnelly, 2010).

Mark Kurlansky, a noted expert on Basque culture and history has made important matters on this very issue, too:

Though numerous attempts have been made, no one has ever found a linguistic relative of Euskera. It is an orphan language that does not even belong to the Indo-European family of languages. This is a remarkable fact because once the Indo-Europeans began their Bronze Age sweep from the Asian subcontinent across Europe, virtually no group, no matter how isolated, was left untouched (Kurlansky, 2001).

Then there are the words of Doron M. Behar, of the Pasteur Institute, Unit of Human Evolutionary Genetics, Department of Genome and Genetics (Paris, France), who says: "The linguistic isolation of the Basques, together with their outlier position with respect to a large set of classical genetic markers, has strengthened the view of Basques as being a genetic isolate with the greatest degree of genetic continuity with the early European, Paleolithic hunter-gatherers" (Behar, 2012).

The reference to the Basques as being a genetic isolate is notable, given the next part of the story of these intriguing and almost-legendary people, which takes matters to an entirely different level.

"The Head Was Not Built Like That of Other Men"

For such a relatively small group of people, the Basques exhibit extraordinary and undeniable traits and characteristics. We have already seen how their language bears little resemblance to any other European language, and is only slightly suggestive of a few linkages to the people of ancient North Africa—and even that theory has been questioned and debated. Most important of all, however, is the Basque connection to the subject matter of this very book: a deeply unusual bloodline, one that may well have at its heart an overwhelming extraterrestrial component.

I mentioned earlier that in the United States, close to 90 percent of the Caucasian population is Rh positive, as is in excess of 90 percent of African Americans, and close to 100 percent of all Asian Americans. Figures are extremely similar for most of the rest of the world. What this all demonstrates is that, on a planet-wide scale, the number of Rh negatives is very small—that is, aside from one particular place where they are absolutely *teeming*: Basque Country, of course.

One of the most important and noticeable things about the Basque people is their physical appearance. It is markedly different from that of their fellow French and Spanish people. Let's start with the head. The chins and jaws of the Basques are far more powerful and sturdy-looking than average. Their earlobes are overly long. Their noses are noticeably prominent, and their eyebrows are bushy—very often to an extreme degree.

In *The Basque History of the World*, Mark Kurlansky quotes the words of an 1880s-era observer of the Basque people, who said: "Someone gave me a Basque body and I dissected it, and I assert that *the head was not built like that of other men*" (emphasis added) (Kurlansky, 2001).

As for the bodies of the Basques, the differences are most obvious in the men: They are generally possessed of muscular chests, wide shoulders, and thick and solid arms. Of course, anyone can bulk up with a dedicated exercise regime and a calorie-loaded diet. For the Basques, however, this is their natural appearance. It was also the appearance of the Cro-Magnons, who lived in the very same, exact area, albeit millennia previously.

Does that mean Cro-Magnon man was, himself, Rh negative? Yes, almost certainly. How can we be so sure? The answer is a simple one: In other areas of the world where today's human population has a higher-than-normal Rh negative figure—such as the Canary Islands and Morocco's Atlas Mountains—Cro-Magnon man just happened to proliferate. The matter of an even earlier lineage for Rh negative individuals—namely, the Cro-Magnons—will be returned to in the next chapter. For now, back to the Basques.

Given the statistics that exist elsewhere in the world, it's remarkable to note that within Basque Country the number of people who are Type O (the one group of blood that can be transfused into anyone, regardless of their own, personal blood group) is around 50 percent. In the Soule region of the Pyrenees, it's closer to 60 percent. All of this is astonishing, given the statistics that exist in the rest of the world. Type A accounts for most of the remainder, while Type B blood, somewhat curiously, is practically unheard of in the Basques. Truly, they are a people set apart from the rest of us.

Now that we have seen how one group of people is, for all intents and purposes, significantly and physically different from the rest of the population, it's time to see how the Basques may have inherited their uniqueness—and their bloodline—from the aforementioned Cro-Magnons. And, in doing so, we will learn how and why it may have been the Cro-Magnons who had the honor—if that's the right term to utilize—of becoming the guinea pigs of a gene-manipulating alien civilization, tens of thousands of years ago.

· The Curious Case of the Cro-Magnons ·

Before we get to the important matter of potential, ancient, genetic manipulation of Cro-Magnon man by advanced, non-human entities, it's first vital to have an understanding and appreciation of who, exactly, the Cro-Magnons were, as well as knowledge of their origins, lives, culture, and history. It was in 1868 that the very first evidence surfaced on this previously unknown, European human. The location of the discovery was a rocky area situated close to the small hamlet of Les Eyzies, situated in Aquitaine, southwestern France. And it was a discovery that was made purely by accident. At the time, the area in question was being extensively modified by the creation of a new roadway. As workers began the task of re-sculpting significant portions of the landscape, a rocky shelter was discovered in a limestone cliff. But, that wasn't all that was discovered. Indeed, what was found within the shelter changed just about everything known at the time about the origin and evolution of the human race.

The shelter extended into a cave-like affair, one that contained the skeletal remains of no less than five individuals—four adults and a child—and a few other bones suggesting the presence of an untold number of others, too. It was clear that these long-dead people were not of a savage, brutish kind: Carefully fashioned jewelry, made out of animal teeth, was found alongside the dead. And the nature and layout of the cave suggested that the long-deceased had been respectfully laid to rest.

Profiling the Cro-Magnons

We have a French 19th-century geologist, Louis Lartet, to thank for kick-starting the research—in the immediate aftermath of the discovery—into what proved to be a startling, near-jaw-dropping find. Lartet was the ideal person to undertake the work; one of the driving forces in the early years of paleontology, he was a prestigious cave excavator, as well as a keen paleontologist. Further research demonstrated that the period in which the people had lived was somewhere in the order of close to 30,000 years ago, which was during the Upper Paleolithic period and which extended to about 10,000 years ago.

It quickly became clear to Lartet's team that, despite the relative sophistication of the Cro-Magnons, this particular group had, over time, suffered from significant, physical trauma. One of the males had been blighted by a widespread fungal infection. A female skeleton bore the classic signs of a considerably fractured skull. There was also damage to the necks of several of the individuals, indicated by the fact that several of their vertebrae had become fused. Clearly, despite being a relatively sophisticated race, one that enjoyed adorning themselves with jewelry and who had a respect for the dead, their lives were far from free of drama and hardships.

Studies of the now-extensive remains of Cro-Magnons demonstrate that they were a formidable body of people: They were olive-skinned, powerfully built, muscular, highly athletic, and, in terms of their height, they towered over other early groups of humans. Most students of Cro-Magnon history suggest that the average, adult male grew to somewhere in the region of around 5'7" to 5'10" in height. Other researchers, however, have suggested—from a study of certain, recovered bones—that Cro-Magnon males may have exceeded 6 feet in height, at least in some cases.

Perhaps most intriguing of all are two notable issues: (1) The Cro-Magnons had a brain capacity that significantly exceeded that of ours today, and (2) their vocal cords did not differ to any meaningful degree from ours. In short, Cro-Magnons could speak and probably had a language. That these ancient people were highly evolved ones, with their own ritualistic behavior, has led to suspicions that they likely had the ability to sing, too. It's important also to note that the Cro-Magnons were not a species distinct and different from us, *Homo sapiens*. They are, in fact, the earliest known example of today's *Homo sapiens*.

Additional studies, coupled with the discovery of further ancient artifacts, have demonstrated that the Cro-Magnons were highly skilled creators of tools and weapons. Items akin to modern-day chisels have been extracted from old Cro-Magnon cave dwellings, as have formidable, animal-killing blades. Other tools appear to have been used to smooth out leather, probably for clothing.

Then there is the matter of how the Cro-Magnons treated their deceased. I have noted how the original find in France was of a group of Cro-Magnons, dead and laid out together. Excavations of additional areas in which the Cro-Magnons lived has shown that they had great respect for the dead, and did not merely dump the bodies of the deceased or leave them in places where they might be devoured by wild animals. No. Instead, great reverence was afforded to the dead, and their bodies were generally buried according to not-entirely-understood rituals, albeit ones of a fairly complex nature.

The Art of Ancient Humans

Still on the matter of rituals, the Cro-Magnons were prestigious and skillful creators of little statues, more than a few of which clearly represented pregnant women. This has led to the probably correct theory that fertility-based rituals and rites were of deep important to the Cro-Magnons. Perhaps most indicative of all of the skills of the Cro-Magnons is an amazing legacy they have left us: incredible cave paintings, which can be found throughout both France and Spain. And we are not talking about simple "stick person"–type figures, but work that easily rivals—and, in some cases, surpasses—that of modern-day artistry. Again, the general consensus is that the creation of the artwork was somehow connected to the Cro-Magnons' ritualistic behaviors and beliefs.

The best, and most astonishing, example of just how incredibly advanced the Cro-Magnons were when it came to the matter of their art can be found at what are called the Lascaux caves. They are located in the village of Montignac, in southwest France. At the very least, the cave paintings are estimated to be in the region of 17,000 years old. We have a man named Marcel Ravidat to thank for making the find, in 1940. At the time, Ravidat, who died in 1995 at the age of 72, was an 18-year-old car mechanic.

Somewhat appropriately for such a mystery filled saga, the story of how Ravidat found the caves remains, to this day, is steeped in intrigue and conflicting claims. One story suggests Ravidat stumbled on the caves while chasing his dog, Robot, who proceeded to run into the caves, forcing Ravidat to follow his faithful hound. Another version of events suggests that Ravidat, along with several of his friends, was on the hunt for an alleged, complex series of underground channels that supposedly led to an old chateau in the area. Regardless of which story is true, the fact is that it *was* Ravidat who made the discovery. It was achieved when the entrance to the caves was revealed in a situation that almost seemed to have been the work of fate itself. A tumultuous storm the previous winter had uprooted a large oak tree in the heavily wooded area, revealing portions of an opening in the ground. Whether it was Robot the dog who first excitedly scampered into the opening or Ravidat himself, we'll likely never know. But it's a given that he and his friends proceeded to widen the hole with their bare hands, something that finally let them descend into the darkened depths.

As fate would also have it, the Cro-Magnon paintings (in excess of 600) and engravings (more than 1,500) had been protected for thousands of years by a dense layer of chalk, which prevented water from entering the cave and thereby saved the priceless imagery from deterioration and destruction. At first, due to the overwhelming darkness, the boys could not see what it was that they had stumbled upon—that is, until the following day, when Ravidat returned with a grease gun that he used as a torch to illuminate the caves. He was stunned into silence by the sight of countless, perfect, artistic renditions of horses, bulls, stags, and other animals, nearly all presented in running, charging, and leaping fashion—and in full color, too.

Cro-Magnon man: a product of alien manipulation.

There is something else, too—actually two things: (1) One of the illustrations in the caves shows a woman wearing an outfit not at all dissimilar to that of today, including pants and a hat, and carrying a small purse-like bag, and (2) at the higher levels of the cave there are holes, which are believed to have acted as supports for wooden crossbeams, allowing the artists to reach the cave ceilings, which extend to a height of around 12 feet. This, alone, demonstrates the skills of the Cro-Magnons.

Aging the Cro-Magnons

As time progressed, so did what was known about the Cro-Magnons. The original, 1868 discovery at Les Eyzies, France, demonstrated that Cro-Magnon man lived at least 30,000 years ago. It's notable, however, that in late 2011, tests were undertaken on the teeth of a baby, whose remains were found in 1964 at the Grotta del Cavallo, Italy. At the time, the teeth were believed to have come from a Neanderthal child. Tests at the England-based Oxford Radiocarbon Accelerator Unit (ORAU) in November 2011, however, proved conclusively that the teeth were Cro-Magnon and not Neanderthal. Not only that, the ORAU studies revealed that the baby lived and died at some point between 43,000 and 45,000 years ago—making the child the earliest-known example of a Cro-Magnon on record. Of course, given that the child had to have had parents, and their parents had parents, too, and so on and so on, the likelihood is that the origins of the Cro-Magnons are ancient in the extreme.

On the matter of those origins, paleontologists and archaeologists conclude that, most likely, the Cro-Magnons had their origins—in earlier, primitive form—in eastern portions of Africa, possibly about 150,000 to 200,000 years ago. This is an important thing to remember, as it dovetails nicely with the story of alien intervention that follows. The most logical scenario is that which posits the ancestors of the Cro-Magnons made their way from east Africa, by way of the Arabian Peninsula, and then splintered off, with some settling in Europe and others in portions of Asia.

There is one more factor relative to the Cro-Magnons that is important to stress—and that may be directly connected to the story that this book tells: Those ancient people had a deep relationship with the stars above, and even had their own sophisticated calendar, one driven by the Cro-Magnon fascination with the heavens.

Worlds Beyond Ours

Much of the groundbreaking work undertaken to understand the connection between the Cro-Magnons and the Universe comes from Dr. Michael Rappenglueck, of Germany's University of Munich. Dr. Rappenglueck has had the good fortune to spend time in the caves in Lascaux, France, and has made some extraordinary discoveries and observations. Put simply, Rappenglueck's work shows that the Cro-Magnon people had a deep affinity with, and knowledge of, the Moon as well as its movements around our very own planet. The doctor's findings were not derived from studying the fantastic animal-based artwork, per se, but rather a series of curious, painted dots that can be seen *around* the artistic renditions. Rappenglueck has made a very persuasive case that the 29 dots in question represented "one for each day of the Moon's 29-day cycle when it runs through its phases in the sky. It was a rhythm of nature that was important to these people" (Whitehouse, 2000).

He added: "The secret of understanding these caves is to understand the people who painted these walls. They painted the sky, but not all of it. Just the parts that were specially important to them" (Ibid.).

In 2000, the BBC's online science editor, Dr. David Whitehouse, had the opportunity to spend time with Rappenglueck in the Lascaux caves and said of the experience: "As I marveled at the spectacle, Dr. Rappenglueck moved ahead of me. 'Here it is,' he said, as he headed down the passage. He was pointing to a line of dots painted half way up the wall. 'Count them.' Below a stunning painting of a deer was a row of 13 dots, ending in a square. 'Why 13?' I asked" (Ibid.).

Rappenglueck's reply was that the 13 dots represented half of the lunar cycle, and he pointed out that right after the 13th dot there appeared an "empty square perhaps symbolically representing the absent Moon" (Ibid.).

Taking into consideration the fact that the Lascaux cave artwork dates back about 30,000 years, this makes the Cro-Magnon calendar the oldest acknowledged lunar calendar in recorded history.

And there's something else, too, that takes us to the next step in this notable story: Within the Lascaux caves, and specifically near the main opening to the caves, there is a finely crafted picture of a bull. Above one of the bull's shoulders is the unmistakable pattern of the constellation of the Pleiades—a star system that, over the decades, has played a significant role in a number of accounts of the UFO variety.

· Did ETs Wipe Out the Neanderthals? ·

If highly advanced extraterrestrials (ETs) *were* responsible for genetically manipulating Cro-Magnons—whether to utilize them as a slave race or to simply see if such an experiment was achievable and controllable—they might very well have had a vested interest in preserving and protecting these unique beings. That might have included ensuring that the Cro-Magnons did not fall foul of other, competing species of human, such as the Neanderthals, who crossed paths with the Cro-Magnons, time-wise. Though this is, of course, speculation, it is a fact that the circumstances surrounding the disappearance of the Neanderthals are steeped in fog-shrouded intrigue and mystery.

It was in 1829, in Engis, in the Belgium province of Liege, that the very first evidence for the existence of the Neanderthal was found. Specifically, a portion of a child's skull was unearthed by a French paleontologist, Philippe Charles Schmerling. It took until the mid-1930s, however, for a determination to be made regarding just how unique and important the remnant actually was. Ultimately, tests placed the age of the skull as somewhere between 30,000 and 70,000 years old. In 1856, nearly 30 years after Schmerling's find, men quarrying in Dusseldorf, Germany's Neander Valley stumbled upon various other bones and—again—pieces of a skull. Again, at first, there was a lack of solid understanding of what they were. Today, however—thanks to the large number of additional discoveries throughout Eurasia—we now know that they came from what became known as Neanderthal man.

In Competition With the Cro-Magnons

Neanderthals of a primitive nature are believed to have originated throughout much of Asia and Europe about 400,000 to 600,000 years ago. It was at the earlier point in time that what ultimately became *Homo sapiens* and the Neanderthals diverged from a common ancestor in Africa. Then, about 200,000 years ago (during the Pleistocene Epoch), what is commonly referred to as Neanderthal man began to flourish. He did so very successfully, before reaching extinction about 40,000 years ago (although some pockets may have continued as late as 24,000 BC), which was the time frame when the Cro-Magnons were flexing their muscles.

Just like the Cro-Magnons, the Neanderthals had a brain capacity that was noticeably in excess of that of the human race of today, and were markedly different in appearance from modern-day man: They grew to heights of about 5'6", had very pronounced noses, had arms that were significantly short in relation to their bodies, and had very muscular, robust upper bodies. Also as with the Cro-Magnons, the Neanderthals had the ability to speak, although to what degree and depth they actually did so will almost certainly never be known. On top of that, Neanderthal man had eyesight that far exceeded that of today's human race.

They were far from being solitary beings—they lived in family environments—and had a lifespan of about 30 years. They had a knowledge of fire and regularly ate cooked vegetables. The Neanderthals also had an understanding of death and its implications—to the extent that the Neanderthals buried their dead in ritualistic fashion. On occasion, however, it was not unknown for them to engage in cannibalism, which almost certainly occurred when a scarcity of food forced them to take drastic actions to survive.

There are good indications that the Neanderthals had a deep appreciation of music. In 1995, what appears to have been nothing less than a primitive type of flute was found in a cave at Divje Babe, an archaeological site in the town of Cerkno, Slovenia. It is a flute made out of the femur (thigh bone) of a bear, which has been refashioned into a flute. That it dates from about 43,000 years ago is highly suggestive that ancient humans liked to play, and listen to, music in very much the same way that we do, today. And the skilled nature of the Neanderthals does not end there.

Rather incredibly, evidence—in the form of tools and weapons—found on Greece's Ionian Islands demonstrates a clear and undeniable presence of Neanderthals on those same islands. So-called "Mousterian" tools, which are wholly unique to the Neanderthals, have been unearthed on the Greek islands of Kefalonia, Zakynthos, and Lefkada, as well as on the island of Crete. If there was a Neanderthal presence on these islands, as all the evidence indicates was the case, then such a thing can only have been achieved by one thing: sailing to the islands. We cannot say how advanced or large the sailing vessels of the Neanderthals were, but the likelihood is they were made of wood, as that would explain the lack of any and all ancient remains in our possession: They would have long rotted away. And on the matter of rotting away, let us now turn our attentions to the curious and mysterious demise of the Neanderthals.

The Mystery of the Neanderthal Extinction

Though the precise date upon which Neanderthal man became no more is not known, there is a general agreement among paleontologists that the time frame was somewhere about 30,000 BC. Several theories have been put forward to explain why the Neanderthals so mysteriously disappeared from the face of the Earth, after having had a presence that extended for hundreds of thousands of years. One theory is that the Neanderthals began to decline in number when the first *Homo sapiens* arrived in Europe, somewhere about 50,000 years ago. In that scenario, it may have been the case that the Neanderthals lacked sufficient numbers to take on—in hostile, face-to-face fashion—the intruding Cro-Magnons. The outcome: The Neanderthals were brutally exterminated, one by one, until they were finally no more. A second scenario suggests that it was not warfare, but a lack of adequate food supplies that spelled the end for the Neanderthals—but not for the more advanced Cro-Magnons, however, who farmed, and possibly even bred animals for food. A third theory suggests that the Neanderthals interbred with *Homo sapiens*, to the extent that the former was eventually genetically absorbed into the latter, and Neanderthal man was gone for good.

All of these theories have one thing in common: They are undeniably problematic. As we have seen—and contrary to popular "cave man"–style imagery—the Neanderthals possessed a language, lived in groups, almost certainly built boats and sailed the seas, enjoyed music, and were rough and tough, little characters. They surely would not have gone down without a fight. After all, they had thrived very nicely for hundreds of thousands of years before the Cro-Magnons were a potential force to be reckoned with. On the matter of a lack of food, the Neanderthals were seasoned farmers, grew and cooked vegetables, and were skilled hunters, too. Why should those skills have suddenly eluded them about 30,000 BC, if they didn't elude the Cro-Magnons in the very same time frame? As for the matter of the Neanderthals possibly breeding with *Homo sapiens* and becoming absorbed, although such a scenario might sound appealing and logical, it lacks scientific backing.

In 2008, the Max Planck Institute for Evolutionary Anthropology (Leipzig, Germany) conducted studies on the DNA of a Neanderthal thigh bone found in a Croatian cave, which dated to about 36,000 BC. Dr. Adrian Briggs, of the Max Planck Institute, said, at the time, of the Cro-Magnons and the Neanderthals: "There's no proof that they saw each other, only that they inhabited the same place at about the same time but I think it's likely that they came across one another (Connor, 2008).

He added:

What we've done is confirm that the mitochondrial DNA of Neanderthals and modern humans was so different that it forms powerful evidence that there was very little if any interbreeding between the two species. We have also got tantalizing evidence that the Neanderthals formed a small population and we can only speculate as to what happened to them. Small population sizes are always more prone to extinction and they have a greater chance of something going wrong (Ibid.).

Dr. Richard Green, who was the brains behind the project, commented: "For the first time, we've built a sequence from ancient DNA that is essentially without error. It is still an open question for the future whether this small group of Neanderthals was a general feature, or was this caused by some bottleneck in their population size that happened late in the game" (Ibid.).

Dr. Briggs's words that the Neanderthals and the Cro-Magnons did not inter-breed and probably never saw each other, strongly suggests it was not violent, warring altercations that ended the lives of the Neanderthals. So, if not a lack of food, not interbreeding, and not tribal warfare, then what was it that led to the demise of the Neanderthals, at a time when the Cro-Magnons were flourishing? Could it have been extraterrestrials, protecting their "stock" of Rh negatives by wiping out the competition—perhaps with a carefully synthesized viral cocktail designed to target Neanderthals but not Cro-Magnons?

We may not, yet, have a solid answer to that question. What we do have, however, is have prime evidence of other, near-inexplicable and sudden extinctions that may not just have been down to the work of cold-hearted Mother Nature.

Were the Neanderthals wiped out by powerful extraterrestrials?

Other Unexplained Extinctions

Up until about 20,000 years ago what is today the United States of America, was home to a huge and varied body of animals, including marauding, giant bears, a multitude of large cats—including cheetahs, mountain lions, and saber-tooth tigers—wooly mammoths, mastodons, horses, and even camels. For thousands of years they lived and thrived there very well. By roughly 8000 BC, however, the vast majority of those animals were no more. They were gone. The overriding question is: Under what circumstances did the near-complete wipeout of these particular animals occur? It's somewhat telling that even among some of the most learned figures within the fields of anthropology, biology, and geology simply cannot answer with any degree of certainty.

The most popular theory is that they were hunted to extinction by the growing presence of the most deadly and destructive creature on the planet: us. What else? It has been suggested that the culprits were what is known as the Clovis people, an early culture that lived in the Clovis, New Mexico, area and who were the ancestors of somewhere in the region of about 80 percent of all Native American people, in both the north and the south. This is an interesting piece of speculation, because the Clovis people used stone tools as weapons, and evidence *has* been found—in fossilized form—that demonstrates they *did* hunt some of the larger mammals that roamed America all those thousands of years ago. Problematic, however, is the fact that the massive number of wipeouts of animal species far outweighs the capability of the Clovis people. There's something else, too: It wasn't just the animals they hunted that disappeared. The Clovis people, themselves, did likewise. They first surfaced in the Clovis area about 9200 BC and were utterly gone—vanished—by roughly 8700 BC. Where they went, nobody knows.

Alien Viruses and a Catastrophic Comet

A somewhat exotic—but also intriguing—theory suggests that when man began to spread across the United States he brought with him killer viruses that were able to jump from human to animal and, in the process, decimate millions of creatures in obscenely short periods of time—something that might explain the massive loss of animal life at the time. It's a theory that is favored by Ross D.E. MacPhee, the curator of vertebrate zoology at New York's American Museum of Natural History. He suspects that a virus or microbe, never previously seen in the United States, was the cause. On the other side of the coin, however, we have evidence of deaths of animals, on a huge scale, occurring practically immediately, which is very *atypical* of viruses. Despite what we see on television shows like *The Walking Dead*, and movies like *World War Z*, viruses do not take hold and wreak havoc and death within seconds or minutes.

An equally exotic theory—one that has also been offered to try to explain the sudden extinction of the dinosaurs 65 million years ago—has been put forward by geologist James Kennett and Allen West, a former geophysicist. They postulate that a huge comet hit our planet, with full, pulverizing form, some 12,900 years ago. Kennett says:

> If you imagine multiple nuclear explosions occurring over wide areas, generating major pressure waves, flash heat waves, knocking down forests. And this led to wildfires over wide areas, with major destruction of the vegetation. The burning over broad areas of the continent would have destroyed the food resources for many of these animals. And, we suggest, that is why the larger animals, preferentially became extinct ("Megabeasts' Sudden Death," 2015).

There is an even more startling theory that may explain these massive, unresolved extinctions that have, at various times, taken out the most mightiest of all creatures—the dinosaurs, of course—as well as North America's massive populations of multiple kinds of animal that were suddenly no more, and also the Neanderthals and the Clovis people. It's a theory that posits in their efforts to protect their growing numbers of Rh negatives, manipulative and merciless ETs unleashed viruses of a distinctly alien kind to ensure that their creations did not fall victim to large and predatory animals and competitive humans.

If such an idea sounds unlikely, it's not. In November 1998, the British media widely reported that data from MI6 (the British equivalent of the U.S. CIA) had learned that Israel was working on a biological weapon that would, and I quote, "only harm Arabs." It was a highly classified project that operated out of a biological institute in Nes Tziyona, the main research and development installation for Israel's secret arsenal of chemical and biological weapons. Of note, Britain's *Sunday Times* newspaper reported on this issue: "The institution is to use the ability of viruses and certain bacteria to alter the DNA inside their host's living cells. The scientists are trying to engineer deadly microorganisms that attack only those bearing the distinctive genes" (Weber, 1998).

And of even greater significance, one scientist deeply knowledge-able of the program, and someone who was only willing to speak *off* the record, said of staff at the facility that they had "succeeded in pinpointing a particular characteristic in the genetic profile of cer-tain Arab communities, particularly the Iraqi people" (Ibid.).

If we, in the 21st century, are working on ways to wipe out only specific groups of people, then the idea that extraterrestrials—far in advance of us—could have achieved similar, tens of thousands of years ago with the Neanderthals, seems not so far-fetched at all.

· Welcome to the World of the Anunnaki ·

In the preceding pages of this book, we have seen highly persuasive data that demonstrates considerable anomalies in relation to human evolution, the nature of human blood, and the baffling rise and fall of various species. We now come to the most important aspect of this millennia-old, twisting tale. If we, today—and particularly so the Rh negatives—are the product of extraterrestrial manipulation, then who, exactly, were the beings that decided to play god with the human race's earliest forms? Why were they so intent on creating new and radically different kinds of people? Where did they come from? Are they still among us?

They are questions that lead us to a legendary, powerful body of entities that have become known as the Anunnaki. They are also questions that take us to the heart of ancient Mesopotamian cultures (including the Sumerians, the Assyrians, and the Babylonians), which can be found in what, today, is southern Iraq and which historians and archaeologists believe, was first settled at some point between 5500 and 4000 BC.

Alien Gods on Planet Earth

More than 400,000 years before a huge deluge devastated the Earth and killed untold millions, a mighty race of legendary beings came to our planet from the heavens above—and, during their time here, brought some form of stability, and even society, to what were extremely primitive human tribes. That was not, however, their original agenda, as we shall soon see. As for the physical descriptions of the Anunnaki, theories vary from giants of 8 to 10 feet tall to bipedal reptiles, with some researchers concluding they may well have been both—the power of shape-shifting allowing them to manifest in various guises.

This particular scenario of the Anunnaki performing a teaching role to the people of Earth was a staple part of Sumerian beliefs and lore, and remains an important piece of historical record. But, who, exactly, were the Anunnaki? The late Lawrence Gardner said of the Anunnaki:

> They were patrons and founders; they were teachers and justices; they were technologists and kingmakers. They were jointly and severally venerated as archons and masters, but there were certainly not idols of religious worship as the ritualistic gods of subsequent cultures became. In fact, the word which was eventually translated to become "worship" was avod, which meant quite simply, "work." The Anunnaki presence may baffle historians, their language may confuse linguists and their advanced techniques may bewilder scientists, but to dismiss them is foolish. The Sumerians have themselves told us precisely who the Anunnaki were, and neither history nor science can prove otherwise (Gardner, 1999).

It's now, with the above in our minds, that we have to turn our attentions to the one man who, more than any other, sought to provide the answers. In doing so, he opened a doorway that leads us directly to the domain of the Rh negatives. His name was Zechariah Sitchin.

Born in 1920 in the Azerbaijan Soviet Socialist Republic, Sitchin studied economics at the University of London and moved to the United States in 1952. He was the author of numerous books on the mysteries of the distant past, including *When Time Began, Divine Encounters,* and *The Lost Realms*. The more and more that Sitchin began to address the nature of, and the legends concerning, the Anunnaki, the more he came to believe they were not gods—or even the emissaries of *a* god—but space-faring extraterrestrials of an incredibly advanced, and infinitely old, civilization, which lived on a planet called Nibiru. Not only that, the Anunnaki had life spans that extended for thousands of years—effectively, in the eyes of man, making them the closest thing one could imagine to being immortal. As for Nibiru, it is, reportedly, a planet that orbits our very own sun, that is different to our own, and that is only visible when its orbit brings it close to the Earth—and perilously close, too—approximately every 3,600 years.

Sitchin's research, coupled with his careful studies of the legends and tales of the Sumerians, led him to believe that the somewhat human-like Anunnaki were here to plunder the Earth of its supply of priceless gold. The Anunnaki were not the equivalents of 17th-century pirates, however, taking what they wanted merely for financial gain. No, the Anunnaki had very different reasons for wanting our gold. They were *dire* reasons, too—something that led the first team of Anunnaki personnel to land on our world, in an exploratory fashion, somewhere in the heart of the Persian Gulf, hundreds of thousands of years ago.

It's important, at this point in the story and before we go any further, that I do something I rarely do: namely, to insert myself into the tale. Relying—solely or partly—on the conclusions of others, particularly when dealing with extremely controversial issues, is not just risky; it's also lazy and dangerous. For that reason, when Michael Pye, the senior acquisitions editor at New Page Books, specifically approached me with the idea of writing this book, I knew that its controversial nature meant I had to go back to the very beginning, to not rely on Sitchin (but, equally, certainly not to ignore him), but to carefully read, review, and digest—*for myself*—the ancient Sumerian stories.

The good news is that the sagas of the people of Sumer have been translated into English, something that provides the reader/ researcher with an incredible and valuable insight into the myths, legends, and history of the people of Mesopotamia. Despite what the naysayers may claim, it is not at all impossible, or even difficult, to interpret the old accounts from an extraterrestrial perspective, rather than from one of supernatural, deity-driven proportions, or of a mythological nature. In fact, it's surprisingly easy. Yes, there are certain things upon which I disagree with Sitchin. There are others where I think he was right on target. But, it's important that I stress to you, the reader, such a position can only be reached by carefully poring over the old tales for oneself and coming to one's own conclusions.

The Secrets of Immortality

One of the two reasons for the Anunnaki wanting to reap the Earth of its gold was the life-extending properties of gold. This brings us to the controversial matter of what has become known as White Powder Gold. Token Rock notes:

> Throughout history, alchemists have sought the elusive Philosopher's Stone, the secret White Powder Gold which would become quite literally a vessel of the "light of life." This secret material was reported to bestow powers of immortality in addition to incredible supernatural powers to those who consumed it. Certain famous mystics, magicians and alchemists of history like Enoch, Thoth and Hermes Trismigestus are known to have perfected the sacred art of creating The Philosophers Stone and their use of the material explains the many legendary supernatural powers ascribed to them ("White Powder of Gold (ORME)," 2010).

Tales of mysterious substances, with the ability to extend human life to massive degrees absolutely *abound* in old world tales. As well as being referred to as the aforementioned Philospher's Stone, it was also known as Manna from Heaven and the Elixir of Life. The people of China have legends of how mercury and jade—subjected to certain, secret alchemical processes—could add countless years to a person's lifespan. In ancient India this enigmatic, immortality-offering substance was called Amrita. It should be noted, too, that the Bible references a number of individuals whose life spans were truly extraordinary: Both Noah and Methuselah were said to have lived for almost 1,000 years—after, perhaps, being provided with White Powder Gold by certain, generous Anunnaki.

Manna: the secret to eternal life.

John 6:50–51 notes of Manna: "This is the bread which comes down out of heaven, so that one may eat of it and not die. 'I am the living bread that came down out of heaven; if anyone eats of this bread, he will live forever; and the bread also which I will give for the life of the world is My flesh'" ("John 6:50," 2015).

It's most intriguing, too, that Psalms 78:24–25 refers to Manna as the bread of angels. All of this strongly suggests that the massive life spans of the Anunnaki were not natural. Like an immortal vampire craving for human blood, the Anunnaki were in constant need of their own, personal "fix" to ensure they did not begin to physically degrade and die at a much younger age than that to which they had become accustomed.

Plundering the Earth to Save an Alien World

Now we come to the second pressing reason why the Earth's gold was perceived as being of such paramount value to the Anunaki. The planet Nibiru shared one particular trait with our world: Its ozone layer was becoming perilously thin and something had to be done about it—and quickly. The U.S. Environmental Protection Agency (EPA) says of our planet's very own ozone layer: "Ozone in the stratosphere, a layer of the atmosphere nine to 31 miles above the Earth, serves as a protective shield, filtering out harmful sun rays, including a type of sunlight called ultraviolet B. Exposure to ultraviolet B has been linked to development of cataracts (eye damage) and skin cancer" ("Repairing the Ozone Layer," 2015).

The EPA also notes: "Scientists have found 'holes' in the ozone layer high above the Earth. The 1990 Clean Air Act has provisions for fixing the holes, but repairs will take a long time" (Ibid.).

Indeed, those repairs *will* take time—if ever complete, even. The problems that we face, today and very likely for countless tomorrows, may well have taxed the finest minds of the Anunnaki, too, albeit more than 400,000 years ago. The late Lloyd Pye—a noted expert on ancient, human anomalies—interpreted Sumerian lore as stating that the grand scheme of the Anunnaki was to secure our gold, turn it into small flakes, and then disperse the absolutely massive amounts of flakes into the atmosphere of Nibiru. Effectively, and in theory, this action would create a planet-wide blanket of gold that would span the entire skies of Nibiru. Thus, in essence, the Anunnaki were intent on patching a leak—as one might, in simple terms, on the tire of a bicycle—and preventing those "harmful sun rays," that the EPA warns us about, from devastating the Anunnaki world and its people (Ibid.).

Such a theory may sound incredible, unlikely, and downright sci-fi-like in nature, but it is not at all implausible. On December 2, 2009, the U.S. House Select Committee on Energy Independence and Global Warming held a hearing on the then-current status of climate science, global warming, and the perils posed by a thinning ozone layer. One of the key figures in the debate was President Obama's science adviser, Dr. John P. Holdren. He suggested that, faced with a degrading atmosphere and a world getting hotter and hotter, certain "pollutants" could be released into the atmosphere, helping, in the process, to offset the effects of global warming and assist in plugging the holes in the thinning ozone layer (Jha, 2009).

Holdren conceded that such a massive, atmosphere-changing operation could provoke "grave side effects," but he added, rather chillingly: "We might get desperate enough to want to use it." Just perhaps, the Anunnaki became that desperate, too—and beyond. Holdren's ideas were a direct outgrowth of the work of legendary physicist Edward Teller. In the 1970s, Teller came up with the ambitious idea of flooding the Earth's upper atmosphere with particles of a variety of heavy metals, including gold, as a means to offer some form of shield-like defense from deadly ozone and radiation. From the Anunnaki of hundreds of thousands of years ago, to Edward Teller of decades past, and to the human race of the 21st century, it seems that it's a case of what goes around comes around (Ibid.).

Now that we have seen how mining gold—as a means to try to save a planet from spiraling into disaster, anarchy, and ultimately extinction—is a feat not at all implausible or unlikely, let's return to the Earth of the past, and the mega-sized, planet-changing program of the Anunnaki.

The Anunnaki Arrival and the Establishment of an Alien Base

One can scarcely begin to imagine the shock, fear, and denial that must have overcome the Anunnaki when it became clear that their home world of Nibiru was not just in trouble, but in absolutely *dire* trouble. This infinitely advanced race had lifespans that practically screamed "immortality," and they were a people for whom extinction was seen as a ridiculous, inconceivable issue. Now, however, and finally, they were face-to-face with their own mortality—as, in the end, each and every one of us is.

Central to the story of the Anunnaki are its ruler, Anu, and his two sons, Enki and Enlil, who came to the Earth on the express orders of Anu, at a time when Nibiru's huge orbit brought it closest to our world—which, in terms of the logistics surrounding a potentially dicey flight to another world, would have made a great deal of sense. It must have been a truly awe-inspiring sight to have seen a vast armada of Anunnaki craft—crewed by hundreds, maybe even thousands, of personnel—leaving their own world far behind them, embarking on a do-or-die mission, and traversing the vastness of space at near-inconceivable speeds to another planet. Finally reaching the Earth, entering its orbit, plunging through the atmosphere, penetrating the clouds, and seeing, for the first time, an unspoiled planet, still unscarred by the plundering of man, was surely awe-inspiring for the Anunnaki, regardless of how advanced as a species they were.

It was the job of Enki and Enlil—soaring across the skies of the Earth in vehicles that would clearly have been far in advance of anything constructed by us today—to seek out a favorable place to make their base of activity, which turned out to be what we once called Mesopotamia. That the place in question became known as E-din, has quite understandably led to a theory that E-din and the biblical Garden of Eden were one and the same. Today, we know Mesopotamia as the Tigris-Euphrates river system, which covers parts of Iran, Syria, Iraq, Turkey, and Kuwait. Reportedly, the mission was both dominated and conflicted by Enki and Enlil's ever-increasing jealousy of each other, as both sought to appease their father and become the number-one, favored son.

Studies suggested that work began—to create vast facilities on a gigantic scale—on what is now portions of the Persian Gulf, with all of the manpower undertaken by the Anunnaki and under the oversight of Marduk, who was Enki's son. From that day onward, and for a period of untold millennia, the huge armada of spacecraft that traveled back and forth from Nibiru to the Earth deposited tens of thousands of Anunnaki into the Middle East, all with one goal in mind: to preserve life on Nibiru, with the help of massive gold deposits mined out of the Earth's terrain, much of which was said to have been undertaken in specifically chosen parts of Africa.

Those doubtful and dubious of such an undeniably fantastic scenario, and who may demand evidence of such mining, should note that in the 1970s the Anglo-American Corporation, a mining consortium based in South Africa, uncovered evidence of ancient mining activity in the country, all of which was estimated to have occurred at least 100,000 years ago—by whom is a question that remains notably unanswered. It's *also* notable that in 1997 Ian Smith, the last prime minister of Rhodesia, which is now Zimbabwe, called South Africa "one of the most richly mineralized parts of our world" ("We Cannot Let DRC Fail," 2015).

To demonstrate just how rich South Africa is, in terms of its gold, in 2002 alone, the country produced no less than 15 percent of the world's entire gold output. Incredibly, additional statistics from that same year—collected and analyzed by the U.S. Geological Survey— show that South Africa commanded slightly more than 50 percent of the planet's gold resources, and almost 40 percent of its reserves. If any race of visiting extraterrestrials wished, in the distant past, to visit the Earth and reap its gold, they could have done no better than to follow the example and lead of the Anunnaki.

Interestingly—even remarkably—the names of a number of ancient Mesopotamian cities correspond with the names of cities in faraway Central America, which suggests that the Anunnaki operations may have been undertaken on a worldwide scale—rather than just in the Middle East and portions of the continent of Africa. For example, Mesopotamia was home to Zuivana. Central America has a Zuivan. The former also has Zalissa, and the latter Xalisco. Then there are Colua and the similarly named Colua-can. Clearly, we are seeing evidence that, in the distant past, and across thousands of miles, there was a connection between two otherwise completely *un*connected parts of the world. The thing that connected both lands and people was very likely the Anunnaki. And, Central America and matters relative to gold and mining are hardly what one could term strange bedfellows.

In 2014, four significant gold deposits were identified in Panama and estimated to be worth around five billion U.S. dollars. Anpanama.com stated:

> ...The Panamanian government has granted in concession most of these deposits and their exploitation is currently in different stages, yet none have passed the stage of mining, which is when the material is excavated. At the moment Minera Panama has under construction the Panama Cobre mine which involves an investment of $6 billion. The Cobre Panama mine will be in production in late 2017 or early 2018. Another major project in gold and silver is Petaquilla Gold, which is currently paralyzed due to financial problems ("Mining Concessions in Panama, 2015).

Revolution in the Ranks and the Creation of a Slave Race for the Anunnaki

Although the gigantic Anunnaki program to systematically seize control of the Earth's gold went ahead as planned—largely due to the fact that there was no one in place to prevent it—it was hardly what could be termed the easiest of all tasks. The process, the logistics, and the manpower—or, rather, the Anunnaki-power—were, collectively, astronomical. Though the gold was mined from the deep veins of various countries across the planet, it all had to be laboriously flown in Anunnaki spacecraft to Mesopotamia, where the immense task of smelting the gold was undertaken in earnest. This was no easy process, not even for the Anunnaki and all their technological skills. They were, after all, working on a planet that wasn't even their own—that is, profoundly unfamiliar territory. It was also a planet that had a radically different, torturous temperature, oxygen levels, and gravity to that of Nibiru—particularly so in the hot climates of Central America, Africa, and Mesopotamia—and that, quite understandably, caused certain health issues for the Anunnaki. The growing antagonism between Enki and Enlil, over how the operation should be overseen, and the issue of who should be at the helm, hardly helped matters to proceed in smooth fashion.

Eventually, things came to a distinct and turbulent head: The untold numbers of workers became tired of the work, both mentally and physically, and dissent in the ranks began to surface—*everywhere*, and to the point where the entire program faced the risk of complete and utter collapse when the teams searching for, digging out, and smelting the gold, downed their tools and things came to a rapid and—for Nibiru—potentially disastrous halt. Such was the nature of the calamitous actions of the workers, Nibiru's ruler, Anu, quickly stepped in and demonstrated his iron-fisted leadership, in no uncertain terms. Clearly, something had to be done, or the entire Anunnaki civilization, culture, history, and world faced irreversible extinction—or mass migration to a world (ours) they were not entirely suited to or satisfied with. Neither option sat well with the Anunnaki.

With Enlil and Enki, Anu came to a decision—a most radical one. There was one thing that the Anunnaki couldn't fail to have noticed when they descended to the Earth, from the skies above, for the very first time: the presence, on what is now Africa, of a race of very primitive humanoids that we, today, call *Homo erectus*. The species surfaced in Africa a little less than two million years ago and is known to have been a hunter-gatherer-type creature that lived in social groups and employed the use of fairly advanced tools and weapons on the vast, scorching plains of what is now Africa. Interestingly, Sitchin's work notes that the Anunnaki referred to *Homo erectus* by a very intriguing name: They called them the Adamu, which, very few surely need to be reminded, is extremely similar to the first man of the Bible, Adam.

And so, to ensure that the mining operations resumed, which are reported to have lasted for somewhere in the region of tens of thousands of years, and that everyone was satisfied with the situation, Anu ordered something remarkable—something destined to sculpt and define our very future as a species. He initiated a program to, effectively, splice Anunnaki genes with those of *Homo erectus* and create nothing less than a slave race that would be tolerant to the atmosphere, temperature, and gravity of the Earth, and that would be guaranteed to be wholly subservient to its more technologically advanced masters and manipulators, the Anunnaki.

If the Anunnaki and *Homo erectus* were so closely connected, DNA-wise, and to the extent that they could be fused into one, this strongly suggests something astounding: that a much older, and still-unknown, alien race possibly seeded much of the Universe in an untold time before even the Anunnaki came to be. To ascribe the very close, genetic compatibility between the Anunnaki and *Homo erectus* to nothing stranger than coincidence is illogical. It's also a case of refusing to see a much bigger, and far older, picture that still largely eludes us.

The very first stage of genetic manipulation of the human race, by aliens from a faraway world—aliens who would ultimately be interpreted by ancient man as gods and who were desperate to save their world from irreversible disaster and destruction—was just about to begin. Nothing would be quite the same, ever again—for the Anunnaki or for us.

· Alien-Human Gene-Splicing
in the Ancient Past ·

According to research and interpretation of ancient Sumerian texts, there was great debate among the Anunnaki hierarchy regarding how, when, and even *if*, attempts should be made to utilize primitive humans in a project to turn them into something radically different from their natural, original form. For far more than a few of the Anunnaki, the issue of creating life was perceived as being something overwhelmingly forbidden, something that fell into the hands of none other than their equivalent of a deity and no one else. In that sense, they were firmly against acting in god-style fashion with the human species, no matter what the cost to their home world of Nibiru might prove to be. This is intriguing because it demonstrates that even if the Anunnaki were our creators, it still does not rule out the possibility of a genuine god having been the *original* creator of life; certainly, the Anunnaki believed in the existence of such a creator, hence their reluctance to dabble with what their same god may have created.

Others of the Anunnaki leadership, however, argued that mutating and changing an *already-existing* species (*Homo erectus*) would not, technically speaking, be considered "creating" something. Indeed, "modifying" or "upgrading" would both be far closer to the mark. After deep consideration, the challenging program of mutating *Homo erectus* was given the green light to go. Red lights, there was not a single one in sight. And, with the project confirmed, we now have to turn our attentions to a significant Sumerian goddess, Ninhursag, the wife of none other than Enki. As well as playing a major role in the entire affair, Ninhursag's ties to the world of genetics and human reproduction offer us a valuable, collective indication that the real story of human origins is a truly astonishing one.

Ninhursag: A Genetics Expert of the Non-Human Kind

Not only was Ninhursag at the forefront of the research and genetic manipulation of what became a radically altered *Homo erectus*, she was also someone who engaged in a wide variety of additional and bizarre experimentation that led to the creation of all manner of obscene and strange creatures, as we shall soon see. But, let's start with what we know for sure about this woman from another world. In Sumerian lore, Ninhursag was a deity of significant and powerful proportions. In English, her name translates to "lady of the sacred mountain." More interesting—and downright intriguing—is the fact that Ninhursag was a goddess associated with fertility—the creation of life, in clearer terms. Even more notable, she was also referred to as the midwife of the gods and as the mother of all children. There are, perhaps, no better combined ways to describe one of the key, instrumental characters who helped to create an entirely new bloodline on the Earth.

So, what we have here is a powerful goddess, one who came down from heaven—which, in reality, was very likely the planet Nibiru—and whom the Sumerians, as well as most of the rest of Mesopotamia, associated directly with fertility, birth, and life. It's no wonder, then, that Sitchin came to the conclusion that far from being a supernatural deity, Ninhursag was an extraterrestrial one with a great knowledge of genetics and how the creatures of the Earth could be altered, manipulated, and, effectively, created anew.

A Menagerie of Monsters

Zechariah Sitchin may very well have been onto something when he opined that, just perhaps, ancient folkloric tales and legends of incredible beasts like harpies, the Minotaur, centaurs, and Cyclops were merely not the stuff of mythology, after all. He offered the engaging theory that they could have been born out of distorted tales of early Anunnaki experiments on all manner of terrestrial life, and not just human. Whether these additional experiments, on other species, were meant to serve any actual, useful purpose—or if they were undertaken, as a first step, to see if the alteration of life on Earth could be achieved, before moving on to *Homo erectus*— remains a matter of deep conjecture and controversy.

Perhaps attempts to create a slave race out of animals were also initially undertaken but failed terribly—not necessarily from the perspective of the manipulation having not yielded an end result, but because the freakish beasts were unable to be controlled and reigned in. If so, perhaps they fled, or were let loose by, their masters and made homes for themselves in the wild woods and high mountains, occasionally being seen, and then becoming part and parcel of the lore surrounding those aforementioned legendary creatures of old. In a worst-case, nightmarish scenario, perhaps the Anunnaki elected to go down a definitively taboo pathway. Just maybe, they chose to try and combine animal and early man into one unholy creation, and *that* led to the development of such tales of amazing beasts in our midst. If such a scenario sounds like something straight out of the likes of H.G. Wells's novel *The Island of Dr. Moreau* or the movie *The Fly*, it's time to think again. Fusing man and beast into one is no longer the domain of science fiction. Science-fact has seized the reins.

Genetic experiments of the freakish kind.

Midway through 2011, it was revealed, to the horror of many, that at futuristic, Frankenstein-like laboratories operated in England by Warwick University; Kings College, London; and Newcastle University, scientists had succeeded in doing something that scientists had no business doing: splicing genetic materials from animals and man into one, hideous breed. The end results were referred to as "admix embryos"—a very down-to-earth term for something so manifestly freakish. And it wasn't something that had only been successfully achieved on a few occasions: It was in excess of *150 times.*

It transpired that the fringe research began in 2008, specifically after the British government passed what was officially titled the

2008 Human Fertilization Embryology Act. This legislation made it legally permissible to dabble with the genes, DNA, cells, and embryos of people and animals—and, if so desired, combine them into one, hideous combination. A working group was created that offered the following recommendations, in relation to such previously uncharted territory:

> The very great majority of experiments present no issues beyond the general use of animals in research and these should proceed under current regulation. A limited number of experiments should be permissible subject to scrutiny by the expert body we recommend; and a very limited range should not be undertaken, at least until the potential consequences are more fully understood (Collins, 2011).

A representative of the Christian Medical Fellowship, Peter Saunders, said, when the British media got hold of the story and splashed it across their pages: "Scientists regulating scientists is worrying because scientists are generally not experts in theology, philosophy and ethics and they often have ideological or financial vested interests in their research. Moreover they do not like to have restrictions placed on their work" ("British Lab Admits of Morphing Humans and Animals Into Hybrids," 2011).

But, certainly the most vocal and damning statement came from Lord David Alton. He said, during a particularly controversial British parliamentary debate, when the news broke:

> I argued in Parliament against the creation of human-animal hybrids as a matter of principle. None of the scientists who appeared before us could give us any justification in terms of treatment. At every stage the justification from scientists has been: if only you allow us to do this, we will find cures for every illness known to mankind. This is emotional blackmail.
>
> Ethically it can never be justifiable—it discredits us as a country. It is dabbling in the grotesque. Of the 80 treatments

and cures which have come about from stem cells, all have come from adult stem cells, not embryonic ones. On moral and ethical grounds this fails; and on scientific and medical ones too. (Brinkmann, 2011).

As amazing as it may sound, perhaps a debate of deeply similar proportions occupied the finest minds of the Anunnaki, albeit hundreds of thousands of years ago, when they were in a race against time to pull Nibiru from the clutches of degradation and destruction.

Seeds, Ribs, and the Beginning of Humankind

Sumerian texts also tell an intriguing story of how human life was brought to the Earth—or, maybe more correctly, how it was deliberately altered and nurtured into something radically different from a far more primal form. The Sumerians held a cherished belief that Enki's seed—which, it is not at all unreasonable to conclude, just might have been his DNA, his sperm, or both—was planted in the ground, which provoked eight plants to grow and bloom. They were not normal plants, however. When Enki dined on the plants he fell seriously ill. When Ninhursag ate them, however, she soon found herself pregnant—to no less than eight Sumerian gods. One of those gods was Ninti, the Sumerian goddess of life, who helped tend Enki after becoming poisoned by the plants. Interestingly, Ninti's specific task was to care for, and cure, the damage that had been done to Enki's ribs.

It's a matter of recorded history that in the Christian Bible, Adam's rib played a major role in the creation of the human race—as it was his priceless rib that effectively birthed Eve. Plus, the matter of the human rib cage is something that has a direct bearing on the Rh negatives of today, as we shall see in a later chapter. Yet again, we see how deeply enmeshed Sumerian culture was with tales of the Anunnaki—perceived as deities by the Sumerians—depositing seeds and bringing forth life. In fact, one can make a good case that the people of Mesopotamia had a near-obsession with matters relative to the generation of life, courtesy of the gods—or ancient astronauts.

There is something else of intrigue: In *Atrahasis*, an 1800 BC Akkadian saga, Ninhursag is portrayed as Ninti, who just happened to be the goddess of the womb. Yes, yet *another* reference to reproduction and the gods. But that's not all. It's an epic tale that dates back to 1646 BC and the reign of Ammi-Saduqa, the great-grandson of the sixth king of Babylon, Hammurabi. In *Atrahasis* the reader is explicitly told that the gods created the human race to specifically work on their behalf, essentially as slaves—which closely mirrors matters relative to the alien Anunnaki agenda, and to an almost identical degree. And there is still more to come.

Atrahasis also tells a fascinating story of how Ninhursag/Nintu created the human race. She took lumps of clay and combined the clay with the blood and the flesh of a murdered god. Then, lo and behold, human life, as we know it, surfaced 10 months later (rather than the nine-months period of today). Looking at the legend of *Atrahasis* today, and from the perspective of scientific advances, this issue of using the blood and flesh of a god—most likely one of the Anunnaki—to engineer a new entity sounds very much like a distorted description of gene-splicing and manipulation of the human race—or, of that fringe research undertaken in England, between 2008 and 2011, to generate something new and diabolical.

Creating the "Herd"

As for where, exactly, the experimentation, to turn primitive *Homo erectus* into a far more powerful, robust, and intelligent slave race, occurred, Sitchin's said: "The genetic manipulations...were conducted by Enki and Ninti in a special facility called, in the Akkadian versions, Bit Shimti—'House where the wind of life is breathed in;' this meaning conveys a pretty accurate idea of what the purpose of the specialized structure, a laboratory, was" (Sitchin, *Genesis Revisited*, 1990).

It should also be noted that manipulating early *Homo erectus* in this particularly laboratory environment and making it Rh negative, and specifically Type O, would have made a great deal of sense to the Anunnaki. There can be very little doubt that the massive slave race that the Anunnaki was intent on building would suffer significant casualties while working in hazardous mining conditions. Mining is, after all, even today, a profoundly dangerous profession. The Anunnaki would surely have recognized this, to the extent that they took certain precautions to protect their workers. In our world, careful steps have to be taken to ensure that when blood transfusions occur, the patient receives the correct type of blood, lest damage and even death occurs by mistakenly transfusing a different blood group. It would, however, have made a great deal of sense for the Anunnaki to have all of the Adama of one blood group, something that would ensure that, in emergency situations, any and all human blood could be used on injured miners—and without any need to have to keep checking the specific, different blood groups of possibly hundreds or thousands of injured workers.

According to lore, a decision was taken that the initial batch of humans—or, perhaps, a "herd" would be a better term, given how the Anunnaki arrogantly viewed their creations—should all be sterile. The last thing that the Anunnaki hierarchy wanted was a sudden outbreak of offspring in the labor force, one that might spiral exponentially and out of control, and in very quick time. This made sense, but it was also somewhat problematic for the Anunnaki. In terms of trying to save their planet, Nibiru, from destruction due to effects of its decaying ozone layer, the Anunnaki only had a limited number of slaves to work with; even their skills could only create so many at any given time—and there was also the time-consuming matter of gestation, birth, and the slaves reaching an age, size, and maturity where they could actually toil endlessly for the gods, so to speak. So, a radical decision was taken. It was a decision that, had it not been taken, would likely have meant the human race, as we know it today, would never have existed.

The Surfacing of Man

Though not all of the Anunnaki were happy about it, the newly mutated *Homo erectus* was yet further still manipulated, this time to ensure that its inability to reproduce was removed—largely as a result of the groundbreaking work of Enki and Ninhursag, the goddess of the womb, both of who were at extreme odds on this particular matter with Enlil. Sitchin hypothesized that, despite differing opinions among the Anunnaki, the program went ahead, chiefly because, despite the concerns, it did make some sense to have a never-ending supply of workers. Male and female Adama DNA was, therefore, combined with Anunnaki DNA; the Adama were then tinkered with, and changed *even more*, and to the point where sterility in the species quickly became a thing of the past. And where did the experiments take place? At the Mesopotamian site of E-din, which the Anunnaki had chosen as their base of operation when they first reached the Earth.

Adama. Adam. Edin. The Garden of Eden. The first real man. The first real woman. Human creation and reproduction. What we may well have here is strong evidence that, thanks to the Anunnaki, and their solely self-serving agenda to create a slave race, hundreds of thousands of years ago in ancient Mesopotamia, the seeds of what ultimately became the biblical saga of Adam and Eve and the Garden of Eden were first sown—and eventually accepted as the literal and gospel truth. No pun intended.

As a result of the actions of the Anunnaki, the natural urge of the slaves to have sex suddenly ensured that their population grew massively and in explosive fashion, and to the point where the Anunnaki were able to sit back and watch as their slave race increased in number, and the work to mine the precious, vital gold that the Anunnaki so desperately sought forged ahead at an even greater level.

There was also another development—quite likely one that had not been foreseen or even considered when the operations first commenced. The female offspring of this new form of creature, in adult form, were far from being animalistic in appearance or nature. They were seen as highly attractive to the male Anunnaki—to such an extent that the latter even took them as both sexual slaves and as wives. It is this development that very probably provoked the writing of the following, famous words of the New International Version of the Bible:

> When human beings began to increase in number on the earth and daughters were born to them, the sons of God saw that the daughters of men were beautiful, and they married any of them they chose. Then the LORD said, "My spirit will not contend with humans forever, for they are mortal; their days will be a hundred and twenty years." The Nephilim were on the earth in those days—and also afterward—when the sons of God went to the daughters of men and had children by them. They were the heroes of old, men of renown ("Genesis 6:2," 2015).

We can make a sound argument that the sons of God were the Anunnaki, working to the orders of their overlord Anu. As for the Nephilim, they may have been part-Anunnaki and part-human— legendary figures, such as Noah and Methuselah (both of whom allegedly lived in excess of 900 years), and even the giant-sized Goliath, who was slain by David. Men of renown would indeed have been most apt titles for these select souls.

And on the matter of God seemingly capping the human lifespan to a maximum of 120 years, this, too, appears to have been something ensured by, yet again, the Anunnaki manipulation of human DNA—to ensure that the human race was unable to achieve states of near-immortality, unless the "gods" one day decided otherwise.

· Colliding Worlds and Nuclear Attack ·

By all accounts, the extensive mining operations of the Anunnaki continued for tens upon tens of thousands of years. Endless number of Adama—from the early, mutated *Homo erectus* to Cro-Magnon man and to us—were used as a slave race, living out their entire, grim lives toiling in the gold mines at the stern orders of extraterrestrials, but ones that were perceived as gods by the trusting, if over-worked, Adama. The program progressed smoothly and with barely a glitch—thanks to the fact that the Anunnaki treated the Adama ruthlessly and callously. It was a case of work or die. The Adama, wisely and understandably, chose to work. And, as we have seen, the Anunnaki exploited and used the female Adama, chiefly for sex. The result: the birth of half-human/half-Anunnaki entities, unique beings that almost certainly provoked the biblical legends of "giants in the earth" and the fabled "men of renown."

Not even the Anunnaki were invulnerable and all-powerful, however. The Anunnaki knew, well in advance, that their extensive mining operations could not go on forever. Indeed, they knew all too well that deep trouble was looming on the horizon. It was trouble that had radical implications for these alien gods. And it all revolved—as in quite literally—around the home world of the Anunnaki.

Planetary Disaster on the Horizon

It's intriguing to note that the ancient Sumerians may have had deep knowledge of the existence of Nibiru, for one specific reason: A study of Sumerian history shows they had a keen appreciation and knowledge of astronomy and they assigned a dozen celestial bodies to the solar system—namely the nine known planets, plus the Sun and our very own Moon. But, wait a minute: That only makes eleven. So, what was the one, elusive body that the Sumerians knew circled above and far, far away? Zecharia Sitchin believed it was Nibiru.

Researchers of the Anunnaki have estimated that Nibiru exists in an orbit way outside of the confines of what we consider to be the Solar System—that's to say, far, far beyond the orbit of the furthest, known planet, Pluto (which, as of 2006, has been downgraded to the status of a dwarf planet). As a result, Nibiru's curious orbit only brings it into close proximity to the Earth once in countless thousands of years. What the Anunnaki knew, but that the Adama did not know, is that Nibiru was due to make a close passing of the Earth around what in our calendar would have been a date of roughly 10,000 BC.

The Anunnaki knew something else, too—something that promised nothing but death and disaster on a massive scale: Nibiru's huge size, and specifically its powerful gravitational field, was destined to wreak untold havoc, disaster, and destruction upon the Earth. No portion of our world would be safe from Nibiru's landscape-destroying wrath. Even the Anunnaki, for all of their power and technology, could not hold sway over the movements of the planets themselves, and so they took emergency steps to protect those of their number that were stationed on Earth.

The idea was for the Anunnaki to take to the heavens in their massive armada of interplanetary spacecraft and circle the globe until the tumultuous events below finally subsided. Then, they would return to a newly scarred, devastated world, and try to pick up the pieces and start over, afresh. As for the fate of the Adama—well, the Anunnaki viewed it as a case of "every man for himself."

The Adama, like every other living creature on the planet, would have to fend for themselves when the Earth became a living nightmare, and as Nibiru's gravity pummeled our planet in shockingly quick time.

Not all of the Anunnaki were happy about condemning the Adama to terrible deaths, ones almost certain to be provoked by massive earthquakes, storms of sizes near-unimaginable, and mega-scale, planet-wide tsunamis. One of those Anunnaki was none other than Enki, which brings us to another central figure in this cataclysmic controversy: Utnapishtim.

Flood Legends and the Secrets of Immortality

For most people, when mention is made of worldwide deluges in the distant past, it immediately conjures up imagery of Noah and his mighty ark, which surfed the turbulent, crashing waves, before coming to rest on what many biblical scholars believe was Turkey's Mount Ararat. Many of a Christian faith are unaware that the Bible story of Noah is actually just one of *dozens and dozens* that can be found all across the globe. This all brings us back to the aforementioned Utnapishtim. He was none other than the Sumerian equivalent of Noah, and someone who the Anunnaki treated as not just one of their genetically created herd—specifically because he was one of those legendary men of renown, of which the Bible tells. He was the product of an Adama and the Anunnaki, and one who was fortunate enough to inherit the massive life spans attributed to the Anunnaki. More than that, there are strong indications that Utnapishtim and Noah were quite possibly one and the same—with the story of Noah born out of the much older Sumerian traditions.

The stories of Utnapishtim and Noah are so incredibly similar that one clearly *has* to be based upon the other. It may come as a surprise to those of the Christian faith—and it may vex them, too—to learn that the sage of Utnapishtim significantly pre-dates the biblical account of Noah, suggesting the latter is an elaboration of the former. In the same way that Christians have the Bible, so the people of Mesopotamia, including the Sumerians, had what is called *The Epic of Gilgamesh*, which is believed to have been written about 6,000 years ago. It's important to note, however, that the story it tells may very well date back much further, possibly to the time when Nibiru was about to pulverize the Earth on a massive, disastrous scale. The Epic of Gilgamesh is presented in the form of a poem and tells the story of Gilgamesh, a powerful Sumerian king who ruled over the city of Uruk. It is a city with origins that are traceable back to approximately 4000 BC, and the remains of which stand east of Euphrates River, which begins in Syria, passes through Iraq and Syria, and emerges in the Persian Gulf.

There are strong indications that Gilgamesh was spawned by the Anunnaki. He was not perceived as a god, but as a demigod—a term that translates as an entity that is part-human and part-deity. Of particular note, Gilgamesh is said to have ruled over Uruk for no less than 126 years, suggesting he inherited certain genetic traits that gave him a life span noticeably, albeit not significantly, longer than what one would normally expect in a human. Of note, too, *The Epic of Gilgamesh* makes it abundantly clear the king and his people knew very well that the gods—the Anunnaki—were renowned for their massive life spans, whereas we, mere mortals, were not. As an example of this, an extract from *The Epic of Gilgamesh* states that it is only the gods who forever reign under the sun: Humankind is not destined for a long life. Further evidence that Gilgamesh was part-Anunnaki comes from studying the *Book of Giants*, an ancient text written at least as far back as 200 BC. It describes—as the title suggests—Gilgamesh as a Goliath-sized man.

It's notable that the portions of *The Epic of Gilgamesh* that focus on Utnapishtim are filled with references to immortality, the ability to stave off the aging process—and even to reversing it. It tells of how King Gilgamesh traveled to find Utnapishtim, who was described as a direct ancestor of the king. Although Gilgamesh undeniably had a longer than normal lifespan, he was no immortal god. At the very most, he was half-Anunnaki/half-human. This, however, was not enough for Gilgamesh. Because Utnapishtim was seemingly immortal, the king demanded the secret that would allow him to live forever. Supposedly, the secrets were hidden in a mysterious plant that was buried deep in the waters of a particular river and that, though not ensuring a life never-ending, had the ability to reverse the aging process, to a degree. Gilgamesh, obsessively fearful of death, did his very best to retrieve the plant, but was thwarted from doing so by a fast-acting snake. One has to wonder if the reference to the snake is a distortion of an Anunnaki—in reptilian, shape-shifted form—denying Gilgamesh immortality. Whatever the truth, the king gave up on his attempts to live forever and returned to Uruk, knowing that he was not destined for a life like the gods. We should not, however, feel sorry for Gilgamesh; after all, he reigned for 126 years, which does not include the unknown number of years he lived *before* he was crowned king. Now, let's take a look at the Gilgamesh-Utnapishtim connection.

Saving the "Seeds" Aboard the Preserver of Life

The Epic of Gilgamesh reveals that it was specifically Enki, of the Anunnaki, who warned Utnapishtim that the world was about to be turned upon its head—and as an extraterrestrial traveler, he (Enki) was in prime place to know. Untold millions were soon to die in a cataclysmic event that would see the waters overwhelm the land, cities destroyed and forever buried beneath new and altered oceans, and the old world gone forever. Enki advised Utnapishtim, in no uncertain terms, to take certain, specific steps to ensure that he (Utnapishtim) and his family survived the oncoming deluge. What were those steps? To do nothing less than construct a huge, mighty boat—one that would have the ability to stave off the disastrous effects of Nibiru's gravitational pull.

There are other parallels, too, to the biblical story of Noah: Utnapishtim, like Noah, had a wife and a family; and in the same way that God instructed Noah to take two by two animals aboard the Ark, so Enki told Utnapishtim to populate his boat with animals—or, rather, that is the interpretation that has been placed on Enki's words. What he actually said was that Utnapishtim should take on-board with him what is described as the seed of all living things. This sounds far *less* like actual, living animals, and far *more* like priceless genetic material that could be used, at a later date, to give new birth to the many species that the flood would undoubtedly wipe out. It must be said that, in practical terms, loading a large ship with the DNA of all animals would be a far easier task than struggling to corral and herd two of every living animal onto an ark.

One notable difference between the Bible and *The Epic of Gilgamesh* is that what is referred to in the former as the Ark is described in the latter as the Preserver of Life, a most apt title, indeed. To say that the Preserver of Life was an impressive craft is an understatement. Constructed out of wood, it was around 200 feet in length, had no less than seven levels, and was built inside a week. One has to wonder if a ship was really all it was. Could it have been some form of advanced, seagoing craft of the Anunnaki? Such a scenario is not at all impossible, because *The Epic of Gilgamesh* states that, although Utnapishtim and the people of his village were the builders of the huge ship, the designer of the Preserver of Life was Enki himself.

Nibiru Moves In for the Kill

We can scarcely begin to visualize the ominous and awful sight of Nibiru, dominating the heavens above—like some cosmic sword of Damocles, as it slowly, step-by-step, got ever closer to the Earth. Clearly, the people of our world—even if they were not fully able to comprehend what was going on—would have been able to view Nibiru long before its presence was able to physically affect the Earth. In view of that, they were surely aware that something was afoot—something that was, correctly, perceived as a distinctly ill omen of things to come—a malignant cancer growing bigger by the moment.

As the months progressed, and as the countdown to a violent confrontation between two worlds became just a matter of weeks, and then only days and hours, overwhelming panic must have gripped human civilization all across the planet, when what began as a pin-prick of light in the distant skies finally revealed itself as a gigantic planet. The rumblings of thunder, minor storms, localized weather anomalies, and small earth tremors—resulting from the first, incoming waves of what would soon be huge, gravitational shifts—soon mutated into cataclysmic events that led to the decimation of much of the planet—perhaps even all of it, when one takes into consideration the *worldwide* proliferation of ancient flood legends that exist.

When Nibiru and the Earth were at their closest points and the skies above were black and fiery, the ground heaved, mountains fell, and new lands surfaced, Utnapishtim was already sailing the waters, along with his family, with his fellow village folk, and with that intriguingly worded seed of all living things. According to *The Epic of Gilgamesh*, the deadly assault on the Earth, by the gravitational might of Nibiru, continued at an unstoppable, destructive pace for 12 days and nights, which was plenty of time for the Earth to be transformed into something that barely resembled the world of old. Such a time frame is more than adequate. After all, in the event of a worldwide, nuclear war, we could do likewise today, but in a matter of mere *minutes*.

Waking Up to a New World

As Nibiru's orbit finally began to take it away from the Earth, and as the effects of its incredible pull receded, and eventually to the point where it no longer had any influence, Utnapishtim had the daunting task of finally taking a careful, tentative look outside. The sight before him, as he peered through a small hatch, must have chilled him to the bone and shocked him to the core. The land was gone. There was nothing but water, except for one other thing: select portions of Mt. Nimush that the waters had not enveloped.

Utnapishtim had no choice but to steer the Preserver of Life, as close as possible, to the portion of the mountain that was not underwater, and then carefully bring it to rest in the shallower waters. At that point, the party exited the ship and made for what was left of the landscape.

Although the specific location of the mountain has not been identified, students of *The Epic of Gilgamesh* conclude that Mt. Nimush is what today is called Pir Omar Gudrun, a near-3,000-meter-high (1.86-miles-high) mountain, situated close to the Kurdistan city of Sulaymaniyah. Also echoing the latter, biblical account of Noah, Utnapishtim dispatched birds to try and find land. They were a dove, a swallow, and a raven. It was the latter that was finally able to see land, when the waters, at last, began to recede. It was time for the rebuilding of planet Earth to begin—something that was, very likely, hampered by attendant, long-lasting side effects provoked by the passing of Nibiru, such as further, massive quakes, floods, and natural disasters—which may have extended for centuries.

There is one more aspect of the flood story that appears in *The Epic of Gilgamesh* that must be noted: As a thank you for following the instructions of Enki, and for carefully maintaining the seed of all living things, both Utnapishtim and his wife were provided with the gift of immortality and a positon of significant standing with the Anunnaki. Should we interpret this to mean that Utnapishtim and his wife were subjected to genetic manipulation by grateful Anunnaki—perhaps via something akin to the administering of White Powder Gold or "Manna from Heaven"—that ensured their longevity? Yes, we should.

Searching for Nibiru

Is there any real, hard evidence that the Earth was ravaged in just such a fashion, all those thousands of years ago? The answer, rather amazingly, is yes. Recall that the Clovis people of the United States vanished about 8700 BC, as did entire species of animal—and in a very short time span, too. Then, there was the theory of geologist James Kennett and geophysicist Allen West that, around 12,900 years ago, a massive comet collided with the Earth, provoking massive devastation and widespread extinction. Just maybe the terrible effects were not due to a comet slamming into the Earth, but were the combined result of Nibiru's disastrously close passing and its attendant gravitational pull.

On a similar path, Whitley Strieber and Art Bell have commented on the curious anomaly of numerous, preserved remains of wooly mammoths, that died more than 10,000 years ago in Siberia and Alaska, and whose lives were snuffed out as a result of sudden and dramatic changes in climate:

> The sudden freezing that killed these animals required much more than a bad storm. It required a storm that was capable of delivering unprecedented levels of extreme cold to the surface and doing it so suddenly that the animals which were caught placidly grazing, did not even have time to look up.... To all appearances they were simply frozen solid where they stood without enough warning to do more than raise their heads (Bell & Strieber, 2004).

It's notable too that the Earth was in a glacial period up until about 10,000 years ago. Combine that with sudden extinctions of mammoths, the wipeout of countless animals in what is now the United States, the evidence of the massive destruction that Kennett and West suggested was caused by a comet, and what we have is undeniable proof of absolute worldwide calamity at some point, thousands of years ago. It was, however, a catastrophe—or a *series* of catastrophes—that occurred recent enough for our ancestors to ensure that memories and stories of these events were passed down from generation to generation. And each and every one of those memories and stories may be directly traceable to the presence of that most unwelcome visitor of them all: Nibiru.

Those who are doubtful of the possibility that unknown planets could exist in our Solar System, and still remain undiscovered, should take careful note of the following. On September 13, 2001, NASA released the following statement:

> Billions of kilometers from Earth, beyond the orbit of Neptune, lies perhaps the most forbidding part of our solar system, a vast realm so cold and dark it sparks a frisson of dread among thoughtful astronauts. The Sun, so cheerful and warming here on Earth, is merely the brightest star in the night sky there. And it's so cold that the atmosphere of Pluto—the only one of the nine planets orbiting so far from the Sun—lies frozen on the ground most of the time....
>
> A spaceship exploring the outer reaches of our solar system could go a long time without seeing much. And, indeed, for most of the past century astronomers figured there was little enough to see: only one small icy planet, Pluto, and its oddball moon Charon. Better perhaps to pass them by and head for a far-away star. But wait! Maybe the outer solar system isn't so dull after all. Lately astronomers have found that the frontier beyond Neptune, far from empty, is swarming with thousands of dark and mysterious objects—enough to make a star-bound explorer pause for a second look ("What Lurks in the Outer Solar System?" 2001).

Four years later, specifically on July 29, 2005, NASA issued a press release titled "10th Planet Discovered." Dr. Mike Brown, of the California Institute of Technology (Caltech), revealed that a new planet had been found in the outer reaches of the Solar System, at a distance estimated to be 97 times farther from the Sun than is the Earth. It was contained within that vast realm that NASA referred to back in 2001 and that is officially known as the Kuiper Belt (named after Gerard Kuiper, a Dutch astronomer who worked at the University of Chicago). Brown explained that its undeniable size, coupled with a comparison to the size of the known worlds in our Solar System, meant that it could only be classed as a planet. It was given the unimaginative name of UB313, but has since been renamed Eris, and it holds the title of being the largest of our Solar

System's dwarf planets. It's extremely unlikely that Eris and Nibiru are one and the same, however, as the size of the newly discovered was shown in 2010 to be somewhat similar in size to Pluto (which is, itself, now classified as a dwarf planet, rather than as a regular planet).

What this discovery does serve to demonstrate, however, is that there are indeed large, orbiting bodies in the outer reaches of our solar system that are still being discovered—and one of them is no less than a planet, Eris. Where there is one planet, there may very well be more, possibly existing in massive orbits around the Sun, and which the finest minds of NASA have yet to detect. That Eris was not found until as late as 2005 is something that leaves the door wide open for still further, amazing discoveries—such as Nibiru.

The Anunnaki Turn on Each Other and Sumer Becomes a Radioactive Hell

As a result of the worldwide chaos provoked by Nibiru's passing, the Anunnaki began, bit-by-bit and across several centuries (which was the equivalent of a blink of an eye to these almost-immortal beings), to splinter. Competing factions, multiple agendas, head-to-head confrontations, and a deep sense that their near-endless reign over the Earth—as well as over its people they, the Anunnaki, had, effectively, molded and created—was nearing its end.

Things reached a disastrous point when those same competing factions did the unthinkable. Seemingly not caring a bit that the scarred Earth was still recovering from the effects of Nibiru's disastrous appearance and the long-term damage that the close approach had caused, Anunnaki turned upon Anunnaki with nothing less than tactical nuclear weapons, as all sides became desperate to maintain control over their particular portions of the planet.

The post-flood world had not only left the human race in a state of shambles, but it also decimated the long-term programs of the Anunnaki, specifically those concerning DNA manipulation, the constant modification of the Rh negatives, and the massive mining operations. Much of Sumer was gone: sunk beneath the waves. On the issue of Sumer, ancient manuscripts describe huge and out of the blue devastation on the fringes of Sumer, which subsequently led to large-scale destruction of the area. Interpreting the following as an ancient description of a nuclear attack is chillingly easy:

> On the land [Sumer] fell a calamity, one unknown to man;
> one that had never been seen before,
> one which could not be withstood.
>
> A great storm from heaven...
>
> A land-annihilating storm...
>
> An evil wind, like a rushing torrent...
>
> A battling storm joined by a scorching heat...
>
> By day it deprived the land of the bright sun, in the evening
> the stars did not shine...
>
> The people, terrified, could hardly breathe;
> the evil wind clutched them, does not grant them another
> day...
>
> Mouths were drenched with blood, heads wallowed in
> blood...
>
> The face was made pale by the Evil Wind.
>
> It caused cities to be desolated, houses to become desolate;
> stalls to become desolate, the sheepfolds to be emptied...
>
> Sumer's rivers it made flow with water that is bitter;
> its cultivated fields grow weeds, its pastures grow
> withering plants (Alford, 1996).

Sodom and Gomorrah: Nuked

Ancient astronaut researchers suggest that it was the Anunnaki nuclear exchanges that provoked the story of the destruction of Sodom and Gomorrah, two cities referenced in the Book of Genesis and that are believed to have been located on the Jordan River.

Supposedly, they were destroyed—via fire and brimstone—by God, who was furious at the evil ways of the people of both cities.

It's notable that in Genesis 19, Lot is visited in Sodom by what are termed "two angels." The story continues: "The two men said to Lot, 'Do you have anyone else here—sons-in-law, sons or daughters, or anyone else in the city who belongs to you? Get them out of here, because we are going to destroy this place. The outcry to the Lord against its people is so great that he has sent us to destroy it'" ("Genesis 19," 2013).

Sodom gets nuked in an Anunnaki war.

This sounds very much like a friendly, advance warning from the Anunnaki of disaster to come, one that paralleled the warnings Enki gave to Utnapishtim about the looming flood. Lot, as a result, led his wife and daughters out of Sodom the following morning, by then terrified of what was soon to come, thanks to constant urging by the "angels." When Lot and his family were gone from Sodom, the Bible tells us:

...the Lord rained down burning sulfur on Sodom and Gomorrah—from the Lord out of the heavens. Thus he overthrew those cities and the entire plain, destroying all those living in the cities—and also the vegetation in the land. But Lot's wife looked back, and she became a pillar of salt. Early the next morning Abraham got up and returned to the place where he had stood before the Lord. He looked down toward Sodom and Gomorrah, toward all the land of the plain, and he saw dense smoke rising from the land, like smoke from a furnace (Ibid.).

A better description of a tactical, nuclear strike, would be hard to find—except, that is, for the one that follows.

Such a scenario has also been suggested for the stories presented in the *Mahabharata*. It is an incredibly ancient Indian epic that tells of what sounds chillingly like the very kinds of nuclear skirmishes that the Anunnaki recklessly indulged in, in the post-flood era. A particularly striking portion of the *Mahabharata* makes for notable reading:

...(it was) a single projectile
Charged with all the power of the Universe.
An incandescent column of smoke and flame
As bright as the thousand suns
Rose in all its splendor...

...it was an unknown weapon,
An iron thunderbolt,
A gigantic messenger of death,
Which reduced to ashes
The entire race of the Vrishnis and the Andhakas.

...The corpses were so burned
As to be unrecognizable.
The hair and nails fell out;
Pottery broke without apparent cause,
And the birds turned white.

After a few hours
All foodstuffs were infected...
....to escape from this fire
The soldiers threw themselves in streams
To wash themselves and their equipment
("Ancient Atomic Knowledge?" 2015).

Then we have this, from that same, ancient text: "Gurkha, flying in his swift and powerful Vimana, hurled against the three cities of the Vrishnis and Andhakas a single projectile charged with all the power of the Universe. An incandescent column of smoke and fire, as brilliant as ten thousand suns, rose in all its splendor. It was the unknown weapon, the iron thunderbolt, a gigantic messenger of death" (Ibid.).

Again, it's not at all difficult to suggest that what is being described here—and based on events that occurred thousands of years ago—is a nuclear exchange between warring forces, and quite possibly Anunnaki attacking Anunnaki. Worse still, E-din—the inspiration for the biblical Garden of Eden—was obliterated, too. This was, without doubt, the straw that broke the camel's back, and steps had to be taken. Facing complete disaster, and possibly even the annihilation of their species, the Anunnaki pulled themselves back from the brink, at the last moment. A decision was taken to regroup and return to Nibiru, and leave the human race, including the unique Rh negatives the Anunnaki had carefully crafted and mutated on so many occasions, to its own devices.

Just maybe, however, not quite all of the Anunnaki left. This brings us to the next, startling stage of the story: the ways and means by which a much smaller unit of Anunnaki remained behind and continued their experimentation—albeit on a reduced scale, and in deep stealth, rather than in the fashion of the pre-deluge days, when they were worshipped as invincible gods by marveling, wide-eyed humans.

· Lilith: An Anunnaki Caretaker ·

If, as may well have been the case, the vast majority of the Anunnaki returned to Nibiru when their crazed, nuclear battles threatened their very existence on Earth, it's not at all impossible that some form of much smaller, caretaker-style groups were left behind—or chose to stay behind. Groups that were intended to continue the genetics-based work that had, by then, been going full-steam ahead for hundreds of thousands of years. If that *was* the case, then in the aftermath of the exodus back to Nibiru, the remaining teams would likely have had to scale down their operations to a massive degree.

The gods of old, that arrogantly commanded the entire planet, and held sway over the world's entire population and its supply of gold, for so many hundreds of thousands of years, were gone—maybe even gone forever. To a degree, those that stayed behind might have been mere shadows of their predecessors. As a result of the nuclear attacks, they may even have been significantly impoverished, relying primarily on cunning and subterfuge, as they sought to keep up their powerful, deity-style imagery—but that, by then, had been reduced to a mere façade of its former glory.

There is a delicious piece of irony in all of this: If the remaining Anunnaki were badly affected by the effects of nuclear war, then their decision to continue with the genetic experiments, and the splicing of species, may not, any longer, have been driven by a desire to continue to create and command entire slave races. It may have been because the Anunnaki found themselves teetering on the edge of a precarious, evolutionary decline and even extinction. In this scenario, they became reliant on our DNA, our eggs, and our sperm, to keep them alive. Indeed, this is very much what appears to be going on in today's "alien abductions." The abductors are often described as weak, sick, ailing entities that need us to help them to beef up their stock. Perhaps, now, we know why: When the Anunnaki viciously turned on one another, it signaled the countdown to a bleak, unhealthy future for the straggling, irradiated survivors who chose not to head back to Nibiru. And, ever since, those same survivors have used our genetic makeup, as they have sought to slowly recover their original status, power, and longevity.

Or, in a different, but still directly connected, scenario, the Anunnaki may have engineered biological robots, or drones, to dutifully and unquestioningly do their work for them, in their long-term absence. Such a possibility is not out of bounds. In fact, it's more than possible, as we shall now see.

Drones of the Gods

One of those who revealed his thoughts on this particular scenario was Lieutenant Colonel Philip Corso, coauthor with William Birnes of the much-debated, and deeply controversial, 1997 book *The Day After Roswell*. The sensational story told of Corso's alleged personal knowledge of the notorious affair that occurred in the summer of 1947, in which a UFO is alleged to have crashed outside of Roswell, New Mexico. Corso claimed that while serving with the U.S. Army, he allegedly helped to advance the United States—both scientifically and militarily—by secretly seeding and feeding certain fantastic technologies found in the craft recovered at Roswell to U.S.-based private industries and defense contractors.

Despite the fact that many have championed Corso as a solid proponent of the idea that extraterrestrials plunged to earth in New Mexico in 1947, in reality Corso was willing to consider something very different. The unusual bodies found within the wreckage of the craft, Corso maintained, were genetically created beings designed to withstand the rigors of space flight, but they were *not* the actual creators of the UFO itself. Right up to the time of his death in 1998, Corso promoted a theory that he believed was all too real: that the U.S. government might *still* have no real idea of who constructed the craft, or who genetically engineered the bodies found aboard or in the vicinity of the wreckage.

Corso's statement is an important one, as it impacts not just Roswell, but also the matter of the small, gray-skinned, black-eyed entities of alien lore: the "Grays." Many witnesses to the so-called Grays have described them as being drone-like; akin to bees and ants, in terms of their near-programmed-like, repetitive activities. The idea that the Grays may not actually be extraterrestrial entities, per se, but are biological robots, created by the Anunnaki—who, for the most part, now remain steadfastly in the background and who have done so since the turbulent, post-flood years—is an attractive and thought-provoking one. It's a theory that gains weight from the fact that, even if the Anunnaki *did* exit our planet for their own world several thousand years ago, we have evidence that some essence of them was still hard at work, still refining bloodlines, still creating new life, still mutating old life, and still ruling the Earth—but via a decidedly strange, and extremely detached, form of proxy.

The late Mac Tonnies was intrigued by the idea of the Grays being the product of something else. He said: "...some reports suggest the Grays are a subservient species, perhaps even genetically engineered drones. The ever-controversial Whitley Strieber has described inert alien bodies coming to life, likening them to 'diving suits' used for dealing directly in the material world" (Tonnies, 2010).

Let's now take a look at the evidence that suggests even if the vast majority of the Anunnaki left the Earth—as in forever—they weren't *completely* gone. We will begin with a truly fear-inducing entity that may well have been one of a certain number of Anunnaki that chose to remain behind when the overall alien population left and may have commanded Colonel Corso's bio-robots, and what Mac Tonnies described as Whitley Strieber's "genetically engineered drones." Her name is Lilith.

Lilith, an alien seductress.

Terror Comes in the Form of the "Night Hag"

Beyond any shadow of doubt, one of the most ominous and sinister of all assumed supernatural entities is Lilith. A predatory, evil creature that has existed since time immemorial, she preys on humans, and is associated with sex, reproduction, the stealing of newborn babies, and the birthing of half-human, half-demonic monstrosities. Lilith is a hideous thing whose origins can be traced back to ancient Mesopotamia and Sumerian lore—which, geographically speaking, is rather notable. That *Lilith*, the word, translates into Hebrew as "night hag," is a good indication of the nature and appearance of this vile creature, which is to be avoided at all costs. She also has an intensely close connection to none other than Adam and the Garden of Eden—and that, as will soon become apparent, quite possibly made her nothing less than a product of the Anunnaki, or even one of them. Before we get to the links concerning Adam and the Anunnaki, however, let's see how the legends of Lilith, the ultimate Judaic demon, began.

Where do the stories of Lilith come from? From none other than the people of Mesopotamia, particularly the Sumerians, and also the Babylonians. Both cultures held strong beliefs in powerful, deadly, manipulative demons that wanted nothing more than to plague, torment, and destroy the human race. Much of the early lore of the Mesopotamian culture held that female demons were particularly fear-inducing. They would steal into the bedrooms of men during the night, mount them, pin them down, and engage in wild intercourse. For the victim—which is an appropriate word to use—the experience was far more terrifying than it was exciting.

One of the most knowledgeable figures when it came to the matter of Mesopotamian legends was Reginald C. Thompson, an English adventurer and explorer whose 1903 book, *Devils and Evil Spirits of Babylonia*, describes a veritable menagerie of hostile, supernatural creatures that the Babylonians lived in deathly fear of. One of those creatures was a female entity of demonic proportions who, with hindsight, sounds very much like the entity that became known as Lilith, even though Thompson does not explicitly describe her as such.

Then there was Joseph McCabe, a Franciscan monk, who died in 1955. He, just like Reginald C. Thompson, spent years poring over ancient texts and doing his utmost to understand the nature of the creatures that so terrified those that lived in Mesopotamia—and particularly the Sumerians, who play such an integral part in the story of the Rh negatives.

McCabe had a particular interest in a pair of highly dangerous demons called Lilu and Lilitu. The clear similarity between their names and that of Lilith are undeniable, suggesting that all three had a connecting, original source—one that, unfortunately, is now lost to the fog of time. McCabe said: "Did a maid show the symptoms of anemia? Obviously Lilu or Lilitu had been busy at night with her body. Did a man or woman have an erotic dream leaving him or her excited and unsatisfied? It was Ardat Lili [the offspring of Lilitu and Lilu]" (McCabe, 1929).

McCabe continued: "Even 'the evil wind, the terrible wind that sets one's hair on end' had its demon. Pictorially they were represented as ferocious beings of animal head and human body: the prototypes of our devil's disciples. Some were so powerful that they were next to gods" (Ibid.).

So, now that we know the origins of Lilith, it's time to take a look at how she became such an integral part of the story that this book tells.

Lilith: The Adam-Anunnaki Connection

There is one reason, and one reason only, why Lilith has been associated with the story of Adam and the Garden of Eden. It's all due to the simple fact that the Bible provides two versions of the creation of man that are in notable conflict with one another. Genesis 1:26–27 tells us that God brought the first man and the first woman into being *together*. The wording is as follows: "Then God said, 'Let us make mankind in our image, in our likeness, so that they may rule over the fish in the sea and the birds in the sky, over the live-stock and all the wild animals, and over all the creatures that move along the ground.' So God created mankind in his own image, in the image of God he created them; male and female he created them" ("Genesis 1," 2013).

Genesis 2, however, tells a very different story; it is one we have already addressed: that of how God supposedly first created *only* Adam, but then elected to anesthetize him and use one of his (Adam's) ribs to fashion a woman. It was, of course, Eve. Clearly, both scenarios cannot be correct. Either both Adam and Eve were created together or Eve followed Adam. Which was it? It can't have been both. Or could it? Possibly, yes. That there were two explana-tions for one of the most significant events in human history—the dawning of the human race—both taxed and worried the minds of early Jewish rabbis, to the extent that they came up with an intriguing explanation to try and rationalize this not insignificant anomaly.

A theory was posited that, in effect, both versions were correct—and for one, specific reason: *Eve was not Adam's first wife.* Jewish teachings suggest that when—as Genesis 1:26–27 tells us—God fash-ioned man and woman together, in unified fashion, he did exactly that. But, though the man was Adam, the woman was not Eve. She was a woman who became Adam's first wife, although she was not identified as such until medieval times, when she was revealed as none other than Lilith. Apparently, Adam—Jewish teachings suggest—was not happy with Lilith and she fled Eden, never to return. Then, as a consequence of that, God provided Adam with a new wife: Eve, born out of Adam's rib. Although the Hebrew Bible does not refer, anywhere, to Lilith as being the first wife of Adam, it does acknowledge the existence of Lilith. Isaiah 34:14 records the details of a number of entities perceived as having demonic origins, and says the following about Lilith:

Her nobles shall be no more, nor shall kings be proclaimed there; all her princes are gone. Her castles shall be overgrown with thorns, her fortresses with thistles and briers. She shall become an abode for jackals and a haunt for ostriches. Wildcats shall meet with desert beasts, satyrs shall call to one another; There shall the Lilith repose, and find for herself a place to rest. There the hoot owl shall nest and lay eggs, hatch them out and gather them in her shadow; There shall the kites assemble, none shall be missing its mate. Look in the book of the LORD and read: No one of these shall be lacking, For the mouth of the LORD has ordered it, and His spirit shall gather them there. It is He who casts the lot for them, and with His hands He marks off their shares of her; They shall possess her forever, and dwell there from generation to generation ("Isaiah Chapter 34," 2002).

The matter of what Isaiah 34:14 refers to as the "hoot owl" is something we shall return to shortly, as it is a most important part of the story (Ibid.).

Adam and Lilith: a Marriage in Strife

Moving on from the days of the Hebrew Bible and the early recorded words on the demonic Lilith, it's now time to see how, and when, the connection between Lilith and Adam really took hold. It all revolves around an ancient work prepared at some point between the eighth and 11th centuries. Exactly by who remains unknown. Its name: *The Alphabet of ben Sirach*. Because the story that the text tells is integral to our understanding of the progression of the alien bloodline, reproduced here are those portions from the old manuscript that demonstrate how Adam and Lilith became so interconnected:

While God created Adam, who was alone, He said, "It is not good for man to be alone." He also created a woman, from the earth, as He had created Adam himself, and called her Lilith. Adam and Lilith immediately began to fight. She said, "I will not lie below," and he said, "I will not lie beneath you, but only on top. For you are fit only to be in the bottom position, while I am to be the superior one." Lilith responded, "We are equal to each other inasmuch as we were both created from the earth." But they would not listen to one another. When Lilith saw this, she pronounced the Ineffable Name and flew away into the air. Adam stood in prayer before his Creator: "Sovereign of the universe!" he said, "the woman you gave me has run away." At once, the Holy One, blessed be He, sent these three angels to bring her back" (Bronznick, 2015).

Today, it seems inconceivable that the relationship between Adam and Lilith should have imploded because she enjoyed being Adam's equal, a free spirit, and someone who had a proactive, taking-the-lead attitude to sex. That, however, is precisely what we are told was the case: Adam took a dim view of his wife being on an equal footing. *The Alphabet of ben Sirach* adds:

Said the Holy One to Adam, "If she agrees to come back, what is made is good. If not, she must permit one hundred of her children to die every day." The angels left God and pursued Lilith, whom they overtook in the midst of the sea, in the mighty waters wherein the Egyptians were destined to drown. They told her God's word, but she did not wish to return. The angels said, "We shall drown you in the sea."...

"Leave me!" she said. "I was created only to cause sickness to infants. If the infant is male, I have dominion over him for eight days after his birth, and if female, for twenty days."...

When the angels heard Lilith's words, they insisted she go back. But she swore to them by the name of the living and eternal God: "Whenever I see you or your names or your forms in an amulet, I will have no power over that infant." She also agreed to have one hundred of her children die every day. Accordingly, every day one hundred demons perish, and for the same reason, we write the angels names on the amulets of young children. When Lilith sees their names, she remembers her oath, and the child recovers" (Ibid.).

So, what we have here, is the anonymous author of *The Alphabet of ben Sirach* using the known legends of Lilith's demonic nature and then combining them with the story of Adam and the creation of the human race. Though many Christians deny the story of Adam having had a wife prior to Eve, there are good indications that the person who penned this controversial tome may well have possessed ancient, archaic knowledge of a secret and inflammatory nature. This brings us to a fascinating issue that I have deliberately withheld until now. Among the old legends of the Sumerians, there is a reference to Lilith also being the wife of our old friend Enlil—one of the central Anunnaki beings that fashioned the human race and provoked the development of the Rh negatives. This issue mandates that we address the legend of Lilith not from a demonic perspective, but from an extraterrestrial position.

Lilith: Wife to the Anunnaki

That Lilith was wed to Enlil is, alone, enough to suggest that she may have been one of the Anunnaki. But things don't end there. They have scarcely begun. Recall that, according to Isaiah 34:14, God ensured that during every 24-hour period, no less than 100 of Lilith's foul offspring should die. The result of God's wrath meant that Lilith was, essentially, placed in a never-ending position of continually having to repopulate her family. And how did she do that? By visiting the homes of unsuspecting, sleeping men and stealing their sperm. There were two means by which Lilith secured the vital ingredient that ensured fertilization and the continuation of her unholy brood. One was for Lilith to engage in sex while her victim was in a state of deep sleep and become pregnant as a result. The other was to scoop up the semen of men that had been masturbating.

Demonologists would suggest—perhaps even demand—that we interpret these scenarios literally. Most people might relegate the development of such stories to nothing stranger than the effects of erotic dreams and folklore. There is another possibility: that Lilith was one of the Anunnaki (or, at the very least, was connected to them by marriage to Enlil). That she chose to stay behind, after the mass exodus back to Nibiru took place, and dutifully performed an unending task of collecting human sperm, in covert fashion in the dead of night. In this scenario, the old legends have a basis in reality, but not with respect to matters demonic.

Lilith may have been nothing less than a convenient metaphor for an ambitious, remaining Anunnaki unit that had the ongoing genetic manipulation of the human species at its heart—a program that, given that the stories of Lilith can only be traced back as far as approximately 2500 BC, began after the majority of the Anunnaki said their goodbyes to the Earth and the Adama. It was, then, just the latest outgrowth of the original experiments, which were undertaken hundreds of thousands of years earlier on *Homo erectus*. It's not at all difficult to envisage how the actions of the remaining Anunnaki—securing human sperm, DNA, and other genetic materials—might have led a superstitious populace to believe it was all the work of a demon-woman with an insatiable appetite for sex.

It's also worth noting that in the Kabbalah we are presented with a scenario that takes place long after the creation of Adam and Eve, in which the two are no longer together. There is a good reason for this: Adam is back in the clutches of Lilith. The two occupy their time by producing offspring of the demonic variety. Or, we might say, of the alien-human hybrid kind. After all, Adam was human. Lilith was wedded to one of the Anunnaki. The words of the Kabbalah, relative to Adam's relationship with Lilith, and specifically after Eve was out of the picture, do indeed conjure up the imagery of inter-species sex.

No one with knowledge of UFO history will fail to note that these ancient stories—of turbulent, traumatic, encounters with supernatural entities in the middle of the night—closely parallel today's accounts of what have famously become known as "alien abduction" experiences, many of which involve men being relieved of their sperm. And, as incredible as it may sound, there is a connection between Lilith of yesteryear and the so-called alien Grays of today's abduction lore.

The UFO-Owl Connection

Isaiah 34:14 says of Lilith that "...the hoot owl shall nest and lay eggs, hatch them out and gather them in her [Lilith's] shadow...." This is most important because there are countless modern-day reports of associations between alien abductions and what are perceived as owls, but that may, in fact, be screen memories for something far stranger. That another ancient name for Lilith is the "screech owl," only serves to amplify the owl connection ("Isaiah Chapter 34," 2015).

Whitley Strieber is the author of what is probably the most widely recognized book on the alien abduction phenomenon. It might actually be the most widely recognized UFO book *ever*: *Communion*, a *New York Times* best-seller, was published in 1987. The cover of Strieber's book displays a near-hypnotic image of an alien Gray. It's surely no coincidence that immediately after the first abduction experience that Strieber recalled, on December 26, 1985, Strieber's mind was filled with owl-based imagery.

Strieber's very own sister had her own experience with an anomalous owl in the early 1960s. Strieber said that as his sister was driving between the Texas towns of Comfort and Kerrville, and after the witching hour had struck, "...she was terrified to see a huge light sail down and cross the road ahead of her. A few minutes later an owl flew in front of the car. I have to wonder if that is not a screen memory, but my sister has no sense of it" (Strieber, 1987).

Strieber has collected other such stories. One concerns a married couple, Doug and Sandy, who, while driving along one of the roads on Hawaii's Big Island, saw what at first glance appeared to be a huge owl that almost collided with their vehicle and that was followed by two specific things: an encounter with a glowing figure and a period of missing time.

An elderly lady named Quinn, a resident of Ontario, Canada, told the late abduction researcher Budd Hopkins that after she, her husband, and their son, had a UFO encounter in 1995, in the Rocky Mountains, they encountered what looked like an owl, but of at least 4 feet in height. Perhaps with a great deal of justification, Quinn told Hopkins: "Personally, I don't think it was an owl; but that is what my mind remembers. That's what my son and spouse remember too" ("Quinn's Story...Profile of an Abductee," 1992).

Such cases absolutely abound in alien abduction lore. But, for our purposes and relevancy to the subject matter in hand, one more will suffice.

A nomalous Owls and Rh Negatives

Mike Clelland is the brains behind the *Hidden Experience* blog. Clelland has experienced numerous strange phenomena—many of a UFO nature and directly connected to owls, and which also provoke thoughts of screen memories. Such is the extent to which Clelland has had these experiences, and has collected a mountain of similar reports from others, he has penned a detailed, excellent paper on the subject titled "Owls and the UFO Abductee." But there is something else that is extremely worth noting, in regards to Clelland and his experiences. He said, in March 2012:

> I just did a home test to determine my blood type. I am A Negative. *That means I am Rh Negative.* If anyone has been following what's going on in the UFO abduction research circles, you'll know that blood type is now one of the questions that gets asked when interviewing a potential abductee. I just went to a UFO conference and *everybody was asking each other about their blood type...* The Rh Negative factor makes up approximately 15% of the world's population. And, according to some researchers, 54% of UFO abductees have the Rh Negative factor (Clelland, 2012).

Clelland added: "Also, my father has O Negative blood, the universal donor" (Ibid.).

•••

In view of all the above, it's essential to ask the questions: Was Lilith, perceived for so long as the definitive, predatory, she-demon, actually nothing of the sort? Why was she so obsessed with collecting human sperm? What of her need to continually create hybrid offspring, and her marriage to Enlil of the Anunnaki and also to Adam? And what of her associations with owls—to the extent that she even became named after one, the "screech owl"? Why so many UFO-owl connections today? All of the issues raised in these questions point us in the direction of an ancient, Anunnaki-driven genetic program that commenced after the main Anunnaki returned home, that continues to this very day, and that employs the use of owl-based screen memories to camouflage what is *really* afoot. Just as it did thousands of years ago, when the demonic meme was embraced by the terrified people of Sumer and Babylonia. Was Lilith, the ultimate, female demon, actually one of the Anunnaki? Don't bet against it.

• Incubus and Succubus •

Connected to the story of Lilith, and to such an extent that they are clearly part of the same overall phenomenon, in some fashion, are the many accounts of encounters with what are termed Incubus and Succubus. The former is a male demon, and the latter is female. Their sexual, predatory attacks on the unwary can be traced back to the legends of the people of Sumer and Babylonia—just as was the case with Lilith, she of the Anunnaki, and once the wife of the Anunnaki-created Adam.

"Incubus" is a very apt title for the male category of these menacing entities, as its origins can be found in the Latin word *incubare*, which translates as "to lie upon." Typically, attacks were—and still are, to this very day—made upon unsuspecting individuals during the early hours of the morning, and most often between 2 a.m. and 4 a.m.—arguably the time when a person is in the throes of deep sleep and, therefore, open and vulnerable to a supernatural assault. Or to an alien intrusion.

It is very important that we take note of the intriguing words of Augustine of Hippo—far better known as St. Augustine, a philosopher who died in 430 AD in what, today, is Algeria. He said of the Incubus/Succubus phenomenon:

Many persons affirm that they have had the experience, or have heard from such as have experienced it, that the Satyrs and Fauns, whom the common folk call incubi, have often presented themselves before women, and have sought and procured intercourse with them. Hence it is folly to deny it. But God's holy angels could not fall in such fashion before the deluge. Hence by the sons of God are to be understood the sons of Seth, who were good; while by the daughters of men the Scripture designates those who sprang from the race of Cain. Nor is it to be wondered at that giants should be born of them; for they were not all giants, albeit there were many more before than after the deluge (Aquinas, 1997).

That, in this particular context, St. Augustine should have made mention of "Satyrs and Fauns"—fabulous beasts of ancient legend—is notable. Why? Very simple: Zechariah Sitchin postulated that the legends of these, as well as other, legendary entities, like the Cyclops, the Centaur, and the Minotaur, were the products of freakish experimentation undertaken by the Anunnaki, all around the time they began to change the genetic makeup of *Homo erectus* (Ibid.).

Bedroom Invaders of the Terrifying Kind

In 1486, a German, Dominican priest, Heinrich Kramer, penned a book titled *Malleus Maleficarum*, which was published in the following year (in English: *The Hammer of Witches*). It's a book that Dr. Paul Chambers, author of *Sex and the Paranormal*, describes as "outstanding and frightening" (Chambers, 1999).

Kramer was a notable figure in the fight against heresy, and someone who lectured widely on his studies of demonology. In the pages of his book, which is essential reading for anyone fascinated by matters relative to the Incubus, the Succubus, and evil, seductive beings, Kramer addresses an issue that keeps cropping up, time and again: the need to collect and make use of human sperm. He wrote: "At first it may truly seem that it is not in accordance with the Catholic Faith to maintain that children can be begotten by devils, that is to say, by Incubi and Succubi: for God Himself, before sin came into the world, instituted human procreation, since He created woman from the rib of man to be a helpmeet unto man" (Summers, 2013).

Kramer, however, felt that the Catholic faith was not seeing what he perceived as a much bigger picture. He added: "But it may be argued that devils take their part in this generation not as the essential cause, but as a secondary and artificial cause, since they busy themselves by interfering with the process of normal copulation and conception, by obtaining human semen, and themselves transferring it" (Ibid.).

Finally, we have these words from Kramer:

Moreover, to beget a child is the act of a living body, but devils cannot bestow life upon the bodies which they assume; because life formally only proceeds from the soul, and the act of generation is the act of the physical organs which have bodily life. Therefore bodies which are assumed in this way cannot either beget or bear. Yet it may be said that these devils assume a body not in order that they may bestow life upon it, but that they may by the means of this body preserve human semen, and pass the semen on to another body (Ibid.).

Again, just as the Anunnaki did tens and hundreds of thousands of years ago, and as Lilith did in ancient Sumer and Babylonia, and at least as far back as 2500 BC, so the Incubi and the Succubi had a program that involved the collection of sperm and the creation of new life that was part-supernatural in nature, due to the non-human nature of these almost parasitic abominations.

From Incubus and Succubus to the Old Hag
Moving on, in a 1900 book, *History of the Devil and the Idea of Evil* written by Dr. Paul Carus, we get to see what some of our ancient

ancestors had to say about the unholy offspring that a coupling between an Incubus and a man, or a Succubus and a woman could create. Carus recorded:

> The theory of incubi and succubi is presented in all its indecency on the authority of St. Thomas Aquinas, who in his commentary on Job (Chap. 40) interprets Behemoth (a large animal, probably the elephant) as the Devil, and derives from the mention of the animal's sexual strength (verse 16) the theory that evil demons can have intercourse with human beings. Satan is supposed to serve first as a succubus (or female devil) to men, and then as an incubus (or male devil) to women; and St. Thomas declares that children begotten in this way ought to be regarded as the children of the men whom Satan served as succubus. They would, however, the more cunning than normal children on account of the demoniacal influence to which they were exposed in their pre-natal condition. Matthæus Paris mentions that within six months one such incubus-baby developed all its teeth and attained the size of a boy of seven years, while his mother became consumptive and died (Carus, 2004).

Clearly, there was something decidedly non-human about the offspring of these terrifying, late-night couplings. As for St. Thomas Aquinas, to whom Carus referred, he was highly knowledgeable on this matter. He said of assaults on the sleeping and the unwary, and of the nature of the children that resulted: "Still, if some are occasionally begotten from demons, it is not from the seed of such demons, nor from their assumed bodies, but from the seed of men, taken for the purpose; as when the demon assumes first the form of a woman, and afterwards of a man; just so they take the seed of other things for other generating purposes" (Ibid.).

One of the biggest problems when it comes to the Incubus and the Succubus is the matter of their physical appearance—or, more correctly, their *multiple* appearances. People who have experienced sleep paralysis have described encounters with the so-called Gray extraterrestrials of UFO/alien abduction lore. Others have claimed literal rape at things that resemble literal, fork-tailed, horned, glowing-eyed demons. More than a few have found themselves under the sway of the closest thing one could imagine to a real-life, shape-shifting, werewolf.

Many have experienced horrifying visitations from a phenomenon called the "Old Hag." It's a creature that surfaces all around the world, but that is most curiously prevalent, for reasons that remain unknown, among the people of Newfoundland, Canada. As its name suggests, this breed of creature manifests as a white-haired, withered and wailing, ancient crone. A welcome visitor, she is not.

All in the Mind?

The prevailing, skeptical view on encounters with an Incubus or a Succubus is that they are provoked by something called hypnagogia, better known as sleep paralysis. It is an age-old phenomenon that was finally given a name in the 19th century by a French physician, Louis Ferdinand Alfred Maury. Essentially, sleep paralysis is a physical state that is somewhere between being awake and being asleep. At that hazy moment, when transition from one distinct state to another is occurring—and, more importantly, if and when that transition is violently interrupted—both body and mind act in decidedly strange fashion.

Sleep paralysis plunges a person into a dream-like condition in which they, literally, cannot move. For all intents and purposes they are physically paralyzed, and that includes their vocal chords: The person is unable to shout, or scream, for help. They also, typically, detect a deeply malevolent presence in the room in which they are sleeping—or, on other occasions, experiencers will describe predatory forms slowly, and in creeping fashion, approaching the room. It's an experience that can be accompanied by strange and menacing voices, incomprehensible words screamed or whispered at the terrified soul in rapid-fire time, and the sense of something dangerous looming over the affected person, as they struggle to both wake up and move. When they finally manage to do so, the dark atmosphere and attendant malevolent entity are gone, practically immediately.

Sleep paralysis: terror in the night.

Those skeptical of the idea that sleep paralysis has external origins would likely say that the large number of Old Hag encounters that originate in Newfoundland are caused by cultural conditioning, and subconscious knowledge of how the experience should play out. Of only one thing can we be certain: When hypnagogia occurs, an absolute multitude of supernatural forms appear out of the ether and subject us to violent, sexual encounters.

It's easy to understand why hypnagogia is perceived as being the cause of attacks of the Incubus and Succubus variety. But, there are important questions that need to be answered. Sleep paralysis is an undeniable, real phenomenon; there is no doubt about that. But, is it a product of the *internal* intricacies of the mind, the dream state, and the subconscious? Maybe not. It might actually be provoked by an *external*, supernatural source—one that can invade our dream states and manipulate them accordingly. What has, for so long, been perceived as a demon, might actually be something more akin to an ancient breed of extraterrestrial, one that has ingeniously camouflaged itself, throughout history, and in various guises, including Lilith, the Old Hag, the Incubus, and the Succubus.

There is probably no better way for such alien entities to prevent their *real* identities—as sperm-, ova-, and DNA-reaping extraterrestrials, intent on constantly manipulating the human bloodline—from becoming known than to pummel us with numerous, conflicting imagery of monsters, the minions of the Devil, and hideous, witchlike hags. It is against the backdrop of this frightening menagerie that the alien works—in deep stealth and cunning subterfuge.

· Fairies, the "Little People," and Human Reproduction ·

In much the same way that there is a connection among human reproduction, sexual encounters, the Adama, the Anunnaki, Lilith, and supernatural encounters that commenced thousands of years ago, so we see a similar trend in Europe during the Middle Ages, and particularly so within Celtic culture. That is particularly important and relevant because, as will now be demonstrated, there is convincing data in-hand that offers a linkage between the Celts and the Basques. That the origins of the Basques can be traced back to the Cro-Magnons, who in turn, have a lineage that directly connects them to the human-manipulating Anunnaki, is highly suggestive of an amazing possibility: that despite having effectively fled the Earth long before Jesus Christ was born, some of the Anunnaki—or entities created by their high-tech, DNA-splicing techniques—elected to stay behind and were still on hand to conduct further genetic experimentation on the human population, in later centuries, and specifically in Celtic regions.

In April 2001, it was revealed that extensive studies undertaken by the University College London (UCL) had determined that the

Basques of Spain and France are the "genetic blood-brothers" of the Irish and the Welsh. The project was overseen by a Professor David Goldstein, who told the BBC: "The project started with our trying to assess whether the Vikings made an important genetic contribution to the population of Orkney" ("Genes Link Celts to Basques," 2001).

Studying the Y chromosomes of those of a Celtic lineage and test subjects from Norway, the team found that the connection was slim, to say the least. When, however, the university staff decided to focus their attentions on the people of Basque Country, they discovered something incredible and groundbreaking. The team, Professor Goldstein explained, found that "there's something quite striking about the Celtic populations, and that is that there's not a lot of genetic variation on the Y-chromosome. On the Y-chromosome the Celtic populations turn out to be statistically indistinguishable from the Basques" (Ibid.).

Perhaps the most important statement of all is this: "We know of no other study that provides direct evidence of a close relationship in the paternal heritage of the Basque- and the Celtic-speaking populations of Britain" (Ibid.).

This is made all the more noteworthy by the fact that, as both this chapter and the next one show, there are more than a few UFO cases on record that have significant bearing upon ancient Celtic lore and on its attendant, Gaelic language, too. In addition, they have a connection not just to the Basques, but also to the matter of Rh negative blood, and particularly so the Type O variety. We'll begin with a trip back to centuries old England, Ireland, Scotland, and Wales—the home of the wee folk, the "little people." In short: the fairies.

An Island of Mysteries

Make even the remotest kind of mention of fairies to most people and doing so will likely provoke imagery of small, dancing, flying, female entities sporting gossamer-like wings. It comes as a surprise to many to learn that that particular imagery—which is mostly reminiscent of benign and friendly Tinkerbell in the tales and adventures of Peter Pan, and which were created by a Scottish author, Sir James Matthew Barrie, and first published in 1902—is relatively new. In times long before Barrie made fairies something that little children all across the world have since become fascinated by, however, there were the *real* fairies. Tinkerbell, they most certainly were not.

Keeping in mind the opening three paragraphs of this chapter, it's worth noting that there is a long and intriguing Celtic history and lore of encounters with fairies that—with hindsight and with a modern-era appreciation of the facts—sound far more like encounters of a genetic, reproductive kind with something that was ominously more than human. Let's take a look at the evidence.

We will start with the 227-square-mile Isle of Man, situated in the Irish Sea and sandwiched squarely between Ireland and Great Britain. Archaeological excavations have conclusively demonstrated that humans were living on the island more than 8,000 years ago. Not surprisingly, then, the isle and its resident people are saturated to the core in magical tales of a paranormal and eerie nature. The folk of the Isle of Man were, for centuries, dominated by tales of one Manannan mac Lir, a god of the seas and after whom the island is directly named. It's interesting to note that Manannan mac Lir possessed a mighty ship, Scuabtuinne, which could traverse the harsh waters around the island without the need for sails. It could even submerge, and then remerge, from the murky depths, all without any harm done to those aboard. In that sense, Scuabtuinne (which translates as "Wave Sweeper") may have been some advanced form of submarine.

Of equal note, Manannan mac Lir was inextricably linked to Isle of Man legends concerning something called the Cauldron of Regeneration. It was, effectively, something that prevented aging, and offered a near-immortal life, not a day of illness, and even the resurrection of the dead. This sounds very much like the kind of technology developed by the Anunnaki—which led primitive humans to perceive them as all-powerful gods, and which may have had some sort of unclear connection to the matter of the legendary, regenerative manna from heaven, and white powder gold. An argument could also be made that Manannan mac Lir's Wave Sweeper was not dissimilar to Utnapishtim's ark-like Preserver of Life.

Interestingly, Welsh folklore tells of the life of a huge giantess named Cymidei Cymeinfoll. In the same way that the giant Anunnaki created a slave civilization, Cymidei Cymeinfoll gave birth to a fighting-fit soldier every one and a half months. She *also* happened to be the guardian of a magical Cauldron of Regeneration. Perhaps her huge size, coupled with her regenerative techniques, are indications of an ancient Anunnaki lineage, which splintered off in Wales, one that may also have had a bearing on the sagas of Manannan mac Lir.

There is another connection, too, revolving around the one thing that, more than any other, was so precious to the Anunnaki: gold. In February 1896, an astonishing collection of priceless artifacts, which dated back to around the first century BC, was found near the Northern Ireland town of Limavady. Purely by chance, the hoard was stumbled on as two men, James Morrow and Thomas Nicholl, ploughed the field. Among the amazing find was a 7-inch-long model of a boat. Constructed out of *gold*, it was intended to appease none other than Manannan mac Lir, the deity who never aged, who came from a world where sickness had been obliterated and where regeneration was a fact of life, and who traveled the planet in a curious, sea-going craft that had no need of wind nor sails.

All of this is made even more curious by the realization that the Isle of Man is steeped in lore of what, from our perspective, today, sounds like high-tech, genetic, manipulation of the local population by advanced, other-world entities.

Beware of the Changelings

The fairies of the Isle of Man—and, indeed, of *everywhere*—were very far removed from what one might be accustomed to seeing on a modern-day Christmas card or on the Disney Channel. Contrary to the belief that fairies grow to barely 5 to 6 inches tall, the creatures of the old island reached heights similar to those of young children—that's to say roughly around 3 feet tall. They were most often described as looking very old, wizened, and even sinister. They dwelled deep underground, in darkened hollows, in mounds that opened up into vast, cavernous, winding regions, and in magical domains where—yet again—aging was non-existent, disease was unknown, and, for all intents and purposes, life seemed to go on forever.

Entranced by the "little people."

In addition to that, the "little people"—like fairies all across the planet—had an obsession with human reproduction. They coldheartedly stole from the people of the Isle of Man newborn babies—usually males—from their cradles, sometimes replacing them with one of their own, magical kind. It was a creature termed a "changeling," most often a fairy baby, but sometimes an ailing, very old fairy. On other occasions, the fairies left effigies, often carved out of wood, and known as the "stock' or the "fetch," that were designed to resemble a baby. In mere days, however, the effigy would degrade, revealing it to be nothing more than the rotted wood of an old tree. It hardly needs saying that none of these replacements offered any kind of comfort to the distraught parents, who just wanted their children returned as soon as possible. Unfortunately, they seldom were—if ever.

There was a very good reason why the fairies were so intent on kidnapping human babies: A staple part of fairy lore tells of how the creatures were very often blighted in their attempts to reproduce, with miscarriages and deformities leading the pack when it came to fairy births. So, they would try to strengthen their stock via the introduction of new blood—ours, to be precise. Generally, the stolen baby would, as an adult, marry into fairy nobility—thereby *strengthening the bloodline of the alien elite*, one might be justified in saying. This issue of the fairies, or the "little people," having serious problems reproducing, and giving birth to deformed babies, may have been directly provoked by their ancestors' exposure to atomic weapons, multiple generations earlier, in the post-flood era.

On this same path of improving the fairy stock, there are numerous tales in centuries-old Celtic lore of men becoming dazzled and entranced by fairies—very often late at night on lonely roads, or in the depths of silent, enchanting woods—and taken to the fairy kingdom where they would engage in sex with female fairies and usually with fairy queens. In 1886, F.S. Wilde, a noted historian on Celtic folklore and mythology, said:

> The queen [of the fairies] is more beautiful than any woman on earth, yet Finvarra [the king of the fairies] loves the mortal woman best, and wiles them down to his fairy palace by

the subtle charm of the fairy music, for no one who has yet heard it can resist its power, and they are fated to belong to the fairies ever after. Their friends mourn for them as dead with much lamentation, but in reality they are leading a joyous life down in the heart of the hill, in the fairy palace with the silver columns and the crystal walls (Wilde, 1992).

When Time Stands Still

Then there is the matter of what we might call "missing time." One thing, more than any other, confirmed an encounter with the fairies: When the person—or, perhaps, "the victim" is a better term to use—who had encountered these magical beings returned to our world, they typically found that days, weeks, or even *years*, had gone by, despite being absolutely certain in their own minds that the passage of time was no more than scarcely a few hours.

A classic example of this is the 13th-century story of one Thomas the Rhymer, a bard of Berwickshire, Scotland. While strolling, alone, one night on the banks of the Leader Water, Thomas was confronted by the most beautiful woman he has ever encountered in his life, sitting atop a huge, white, horse. Her hair was golden, and her green cloak was adorned with priceless, sparkling jewels. She introduced herself as none other than the queen of the fairies. Thomas, practically hypnotized by her beauty, asked for a kiss. The queen agreed, but demanded that, in return, Thomas must travel with her to the fairy kingdom, where he will serve her—a euphemism for sex. He eagerly agreed, not surprisingly. For Thomas, it seemed that no more than three days has passed when he was returned to our world. He was, however, terrified to find that no less than seven years have elapsed. So smitten was he by the queen—who had given him the gift of prophecy—Thomas eventually returned to the fairy realm to live out the rest of his days, perhaps no longer able to relate to our world, after seeing what lies beyond the veil.

A similar story, from the 19th century, tells of two Welshmen, Llewellyn and Rhys, who were walking to their homes late one night when they heard the sound of enchanting, hypnotic music. Rhys was entranced by it, but Llewellyn was not: He knew it was the chilling calling card of the fairies, and that listening to the music for too long would lead one to fall under the spell of the "little people." Rhys refused to budge; Llewellyn fled. On the following day, Llewellyn tentatively returned to the scene and found, to his amazement and concern, Rhys wildly dancing in what was termed "a fairy circle"—a flattened, circular area of ground not dissimilar to one of today's "crop circles." Despite the passing of a day, Rhys was sure he had only been dancing for mere minutes.

Though many might scoff at the idea that literal fairies really exist—or did exist, centuries long gone—there is another factor that comes into play here. The issue of small, diminutive entities, of a supernatural nature, displaying a somewhat morbid obsession with newborn babies and human reproduction, and who have the ability to leave the targeted individual with a distinct sense of "missing time," are staple factors of what have become known today as "alien abductions."

Just perhaps, what were perceived as the wee folk, fairies, goblins, pixies, elves—the list of names goes on and on—were actually extraterrestrials, or perhaps, Anunnaki-created worker-drones, unendingly distilling, synthesizing, and manipulating human bloodlines and, in the process, giving birth to legends of the baby-stealing little people of some supernatural realm.

It's now for us to take a big step forward to the 20th century and what appears to be evidence of modern-day activities of the Anunnaki, but with distinct links to the past.

11

• The Anunnaki and the CIA •

Truman Bethurum was a Californian, born in 1898, who spent much of his early years working jobs that never seemed to last. His first marriage both began and crumbled during the Second World War. He entered into a second marriage only several months after the war ended, and ultimately wound up working in the harsh, hot deserts of Nevada—specifically in the highway construction game. It was while Bethurum was out in the desert, in 1952, and while his second wife, Mary, was stuck at home in Santa Barbara, California, that Bethurum claimed he had an extremely close encounter with extraterrestrials on Mormon Mesa, a near-2,000-foot-high mount in Nevada's Moapa Valley.

On the fateful night in question, and after the working day was over, Bethurum climbed the mountain, primarily to search for shells, something that Mary particularly enjoyed collecting. The story goes that Bethurum was rendered into a strange, altered state of mind, during which advanced aliens suddenly manifested before him, having arrived in a huge, gleaming, flying saucer. Although only around 5 feet in height, the aliens were eerily human-looking and claimed to come from a faraway planet called Clarion. Not only that, their leader was one Captain Aura Rhanes, a shapely, Pamela

Anderson–type that Bethurum described as being "tops in shapeliness and beauty." All thoughts of Mary—back in Santa Barbara—were suddenly gone from Bethurum's mind (Bethurum, 1954).

Bethurum's story continued and grew at a steady and controversial pace, as did his relationship with the flirty Captain Rhanes. Although Bethurum does not explicitly say so, there are more than a few nuggets of data in Bethurum's collective work that suggests on a couple of occasions the pair had just about the closest and most intimate encounters of all. It's hardly surprising that many students of Ufology outright dismiss Bethurum's story as either a hoax, or a fantasy born out of Bethurum's unhappiness with both wife number one and two. There is, however, a very intriguing aspect of the Bethurum affair that is seldom touched upon or even noted.

One person who *did* take note of it was Whitley Strieber, whose 1987 best-selling book, *Communion*, brought the world of alien abductions to a massive, mainstream audience. During the course of investigating his experiences that prompted him to write *Communion*, Strieber discovered something remarkable: The name Aura Rhanes was extremely similar to *Aerach Reann*, a Gaelic term that translates approximately to "heavenly body of air." It must be said to that the fashion by which Bethurum became entranced by Aura Rhanes mirrors to an almost identical degree with those centuries-old cases of hapless and helpless Gaelic men falling under the spell of the fairy queen, as described in the previous chapter (Strieber, 1987).

And the links didn't end there.

U. S. Government Knowledge of the Anunnaki?

It's worth noting that in the very same time frame that the affair of Truman Bethurum was playing out ("affair," quite possibly, being a very appropriate word), the CIA was closely and secretly watching certain developments in central Africa, specifically in what until the 1960s was termed the Belgian Congo. Echoing how the Anunnaki were mining for gold in Africa hundreds of thousands of years ago, in 1915 a man named Robert Rich Sharp discovered a huge vein of uranium at a mine in the town of Shinkolobwe, in the Congo. "Huge" only barely fits the bill: Edgar Sengier, the Belgian director of the Union Miniere du Haut Katanga mining company, secured no less than 4,200 tons of uranium from the massive vein that extended for more than 400 kilometers (almost 250 miles).

Such was the quality of the uranium, it was used extensively in the U.S. government's Manhattan Project to develop the atomic bomb at the height of the Second World War. Overseeing the uranium production at Oak Ridge, Tennessee, was Major General Kenneth Nichols. He said of the uranium deposits in the Belgian Congo: "Our best source, the Shinkolobwe mine, represented a freak occurrence in nature. It contained a tremendously rich lode of uranium pitchblende. Nothing like it has ever again been found" (Nichols, 1987).

What does the CIA know of the Anunnaki?

All of this brings us back to 1952, the CIA, and flying saucers. A CIA document of August 16, 1952, reveals:

> Recently, two fiery disks were sighted over the uranium mines located in the southern part of the Belgian Congo in the Elizabethville district, east of the Luapula River which connects the Meru and Bangweolo lakes. The disks glided in elegant curves and changed their position many times, so that from below they sometimes appeared as plates, ovals, and simply lines. Suddenly, both disks hovered in one spot and then took off in a unique zigzag flight to the northeast. A penetrating hissing and buzzing sound was audible to the on-lookers below. The whole performance lasted from 10 to 12 minutes (Central Intelligence Agency, 1952).

The story continued that a Commander Pierre, who operated out of a nearby airstrip called Elizabethville, and to whose attention the presence of the UFOs had been brought, raced to his fighter plane and was soon in the skies, in hot pursuit. Incredibly, Pierre actually managed to close in on one of the craft, to a perilously close 120 meters (.075 miles). In such dicey, near proximity, Pierre was able to get a good look at the object before him. It was, he said, somewhere between 12 and 15 meters (39–49 feet) in diameter, shaped like a "discus," and aluminum-like color. It had an "inner core" that remained completely still, while its outer rim was aflame and spinning, something that led the commander to conclude that the UFO must have had an enormous speed of rotation (Ibid.).

The movements of the UFOs made it clear to Pierre that what he was seeing was not secret, prototype aircraft: They traveled both horizontally and vertically, their elevation went from 800 to 1,000 meters (approximately .5–.62 miles) in barely a second or two, and, at one point they even dramatically dropped to heights of barely 60 feet above the trees surrounding the mine. Due to the devastating effects of incredible G-forces that such maneuvers would have had on a pilot, Pierre could only conclude that the vehicles were remotely flown—by whom, he had no idea. The chase came to an end when, after about 15 minutes, both UFOs suddenly made loud, piercing whistling noises and accelerated to what Pierre concludes was around 1,500 kilometers per hour (932 miles per hour) and were gone from view in an instant.

Whereas the report itself is an undeniable standout one, it's what happened after the report reached the CIA that is far more interesting—and of relevance to the story of the Anunnaki and the genetic manipulation of the human race: The documentation—along with a freshly written report from Commander Pierre—were studied very closely by personnel from the CIA's Office of Scientific Intelligence (OSI). They came to three, notable conclusions: (1) Commander Pierre was a first-class witness; (2) there seemed to be no reason to doubt his testimony, given his very close proximity to one of the UFOs; and (3) a study should be initiated to determine how many more mines in Africa were associated with sightings of UFOs. Interestingly, for reasons that are not clear, the OSI recommended that the study should also encompass sightings of UFOs in the vicinity of *gold mines in Africa*. Did someone in the CIA, even as early as the formative years of the 1950s, know something of the Anunnaki's ancient links with Africa, gold, and mining programs? If so, were they concerned the Anunnaki were now back, among us once again, and checking out *our* very own mining operations in those areas of the globe they once dominated, all of those millennia earlier?

And there's one more thing to note on this most curious, but fascinating issue.

Crash go the Space Gods

For decades, rumors have circulated to the effect that, in early 1952, a UFO crashed on the Norwegian island of Spitzbergen. Tales of crashed UFOs, secretly recovered along with the remains of their dead crews, abound in Ufology. What's particularly fascinating about the Spitzbergen case is that the craft itself—allegedly secretly donated to U.S. military personnel by the Norwegian government—was reportedly transported to Kentucky, specifically Fort Knox. A U.S. Army installation, Fort Knox is also home to the United States Bullion Depository (USBD), which in turn is home to the nation's supply of gold—which amounts to around 3 percent of all the gold ever refined by man, throughout recorded history. Such is the scale and value of the massive gold holdings at the USBD, the current, combined value of the gold is estimated to be around $380 billion.

So, we have a very curious situation here: We have the Truman Bethurum affair of 1952, a case that has significant links to matters of a Celtic nature—the Celts having a lineage that ties them to the Basques and, further back in time, to the genetically manipulated Cro-Magnons. In that same year, specifically that summer, the CIA recommends that careful attention should be paid to reports of UFO activity in the vicinity of African gold mines. And, on top of that, and *also* in 1952, the remains of a crashed UFO are reportedly secretly shipped to Fort Knox. Should we consider the incredible possibility that the Spitzbergen craft contained significant amounts of Anunnaki gold on-board? Possibly, yes. If such a find was made, that may well have prompted the CIA to look for additional reports of UFOs seen in the vicinity of mining activity—and particularly gold-mining.

· Close Encounters of the Celtic Kind ·

In the very same time frame that Truman Bethurum was under the hypnotic spell of the fairy-like and Celtic-named Aura Rhanes, a man named George Adamski was claiming amazing encounters with human-like extraterrestrials in the deserts of California. There's no doubt that Adamski was, and still is, the ultimate Contactee—regardless of what one might make of his claimed experiences with the long-haired, human-looking "Space Brothers," as he termed them. What is particularly interesting is that one of Adamski's alleged brothers from the stars was named FirKon.

Strieber says of this: "*Fir* or *fear* when used as a prefix means 'man,' and Conn, meaning 'Head,' is the name of a seventh-century Irish king whose son, tradition tells us, was abducted by a beautiful lady in a flying craft. FirKon means, in Gaelic, 'man of Conn'" (Strieber, 1987).

A Brazilian Bloodline

It's now time to turn our attentions to one of the most controversial of all alien encounters, one that has notable implications for the Gaelic-UFO connection. On February 22, 1958, a young

Brazilian farmer named Antonio Villas Boas prepared for a Dr. Olavo Fontes—both a respected gastroenterologist at the National School of Medicine in Rio de Janeiro and a highly dedicated flying saucer investigator—a remarkable, and undeniably sensational, document that told of his (Villas Boas's) close encounter with an alien only eight days earlier. But, this was no sterile "take me to your leader"–style experience involving bug-eyed, spindly creatures with an interest in Villas Boas's rectum. No. According to the 23-year-old farmer, he went where, quite possibly, no man had ever gone before. So Villas Boas told Fontes, he did nothing less than get it on with a hot babe from the great and mysterious beyond:

> "I live with my family on a farm which we own, near the town of Francisco de Sales, in the state of Minas Gerais, close to the border with the state of Sao Paulo," Villas Boas told Fontes as he began his torrid tale of sex from the stars. It all went down on the night of October 5, the man himself explained, when he encountered "a very white light, and I don't know where it came from. It was as though it came from high up above, like the light of a car head-lamp shining downwards spreading its light all around...it finally went out and did not return" (Villas Boas, 1958).

Well, not for long, anyway.

Barely a week later, the same lighted object—or, at the very least, a near-identical one—appeared over the farm while Villas Boas was chilling out on the family's tractor after a hard day and night toiling in the field. Looking somewhat like a cartwheel and hovering about 300 feet from the ground, it bathed the area with a bright red glow for a few moments that, even from a distance of more than a hundred feet, made Villas Boas's eyes sting like crazy. Suddenly it was gone—or its lights were extinguished and it was now hovering in complete silence and darkness. But the main act was about to come (as, so it transpired, was Villas Boas). Twenty-four hours later, Villas Boas was still toiling hard in the field when, in his own words, "At precisely 1 a.m., I suddenly saw a red star in the sky.... In a few moments it had grown into a very luminous, egg-shaped object, flying towards me at a terrific speed. It was moving so fast that it was above the tractor before I had time to think what I should do" (Ibid.).

It was all an amazed Villas Boas could do to stare in complete awe at the craft above him. That awe turned to cold fear when the vehicle descended to a height of maybe now more than 75 feet, at which point Villas Boas wisely thought his best course of action was to run like hell and to get as far away from the whatever-it-was as possible. Unfortunately—or, perhaps, fortunately—it didn't quite work out like that.

"It came nearer and nearer," said Villas Boas, who added: "I was now able to see it was a strange machine, rather rounded in shape, and surrounded by little purplish lights...[it] was like a large elongated egg with three metal spurs in front.... On the upper part of the machine there was something which was revolving at great speed and also giving off a powerful fluorescent reddish light" (Ibid.).

It might not seem much right now, but as the story progresses, Villas Boas's description of the craft takes on new, and highly profound, significance.

Still thinking of running to the safety of the farmhouse, Villas Boas's course of action was brought to a sudden halt when he found himself feeling dizzy, groggy, and disoriented. Villas Boas was in a state of quickly escalating incapacitation. He managed to make it just a few dozen yards before powerful hands grabbed him by the arm. Terror-stricken, Villas Boas found himself face to face with a human-looking individual about 5 feet in height and dressed in a flight-suit-type outfit. As for the craft, it was sitting a short distance away and still emitting its powerful, blinding lights, which semi-obscured its specific shape—something that may have been a deliberate action to hide its real identity, as will soon be revealed. Adrenalized and scared, Villas Boas tried to lash out, to no avail. By then, feeling very unsteady on his feet and drunk as a skunk, he was quickly overpowered as three other characters raced out of the craft to help their comrade. Worse: They proceeded to drag him toward the brilliantly lit craft. Not a good sign.

After the four men finally managed to haul Villas Boas inside the very cramped confines, they rapidly removed his clothing and shoved him into a small room, and he found himself covered, head-to-foot, in what sounds like several bottles of shower-gel. Then, after Villas Boas was hosed down, a blood sample was taken from his chin, after which he was taken to another, equally small room—actually, this one was almost closet-like—that, alarmingly, was quickly filled with dense smog that had him gasping for air. In Villas Boas's own words: "It was as though I was breathing a thick smoke that was suffocating me, and it gave the effect of painted cloth burning.... I did not feel well and the nausea increased so much that I ended up vomiting" (Ibid.).

"A Good Stallion to Improve Their Own Stock"

Thankfully, and finally, after what seemed like a torturously long wait, there was light at the end of the tunnel. Very welcome light, indeed. We're talking about a close encounter. Not of the first, second, or even third kind, mind you. It was one thing to get nabbed by aliens, taken on-board their craft, and hosed down like a muddy, old car. It was quite another to get rewarded after that traumatic experience with a fine and tasty piece of extraterrestrial ass. But, Villas Boas told Fontes, that's *exactly* what happened. A metal door opened, and in walked a naked woman. At this stage, it's perhaps best to get the lowdown from the man of the hour:

> Her eyes were large and blue, more elongated than round, being slanted outwards...the cheekbones were very high... her lips were very thin, hardly visible...her body was much more beautiful than that of any woman I have ever known before. It was slim, with high and well-separated breasts, thin waist and small stomach, wide hips and large thighs...

another thing that I noted was that her hair in the armpits and in another place was very red, almost the color of blood (Ibid.).

And it was what he tactfully, and almost engagingly innocently, referred to as "another place" that Villas Boas had his sights set on. He didn't have to wait long, however, nor did he have to break the ice with a bit of meaningless chatter. The seemingly real-life Barbarella was decidedly proactive and on him in a flash:

She came toward me silently, looking at me with the expression of someone wanting something, and she embraced me suddenly and began to rub her head from side to side against my face. I became uncontrollably excited, sexually, a thing that had never happened to me before. I ended up by forgetting everything, and I caught hold of the woman, responded to her caresses with other and greater caresses. Some of the grunts that I heard coming from that woman's mouth at certain moments nearly spoilt everything, giving the disagreeable impression that I was with an animal. Finally, she was tired and breathing rapidly. I was still keen, but she was now refusing, trying to escape, to avoid me, to finish with it all (Ibid.).

Evidently, although Villas Boas wasn't exactly enamored of the woman's animalistic vocalizations, he clearly considered himself to be quite the stud-muffin, as he told Fontes: "That was what they wanted of me—a good stallion to improve their own stock" (Ibid.).

Perhaps as a way of convincing Villas Boas that his friend with benefits was not of this Earth, he explained that as the woman moved to exit the room "she turned to me, pointed at her belly and then pointed toward me and with a smile she finally pointed towards the sky—I think it was in the direction of the south." Then, after a quick tour of the craft—during which Villas Boas was sternly admonished by one of the crew members for trying to steal a small device to take home—he was unceremoniously escorted off the craft, and watched as it, and his grunting girl from another galaxy, left for pastures new (Ibid.).

As Villas Boas recalled to Fontes:

The craft continued to rise slowly into the air until it had reached a height of some 30 to 50 meters.... The whirring noise of the air being displaced became much more intense and the revolving dish [that sat atop the object] began to turn at a fearful speed.... At that moment, the machine suddenly changed direction, with an abrupt movement, making a louder noise, a sort of "beat." Then, listing slightly to one side, that strange machine shot off like a bullet towards the south, at such a speed that it was gone from sight in a few seconds. Then I went back to my tractor. I left the craft at roughly 5:30 in the morning, having entered it at 1:15 in the early hours. So I had been there for four hours and fifteen minutes. A very long time indeed (Ibid.).

It was all over. The aliens had come and gone. Or, at least, one of them had, thanks to Villas Boas, that "good stallion." It was an event that the man himself—who went on to become a well-respected lawyer—maintained happened exactly as he described it until his dying day, which happened to be in 1992, at the unfortunately very young age of only 58 (Ibid.).

Just as is the case with the accounts of Truman Bethurum, Antonio Villas Boas's is one that requires us to almost suspend belief. On the other hand, consider these two factors: (1) The fiery red hair of Villas Boas' spacewoman was, and is, typical of the red-haired Celtic people, and (2) throughout all of South America, the highest levels of people who are Type O negative just happen to be the Brazilians. One has to wonder: Was Antonio Villas Boas Type O negative? If he was, perhaps this explains why he was chosen: to mate with a being that was also Type O negative and who may, herself, have been born out of alien gene-tampering.

Breakfast With the Aliens

In April 1961, a UFO encounter occurred in Wisconsin that many researchers of the flying saucer phenomenon have seen fit to relegate to the domains of hoaxing and fantasy. It just might have been something else—something that takes us back to those enigmatic entities of the Isle of Man and Celtic lore. It was the morning of April 18th and the breakfast of a man named Joe Simonton was about to be rudely interrupted by visitors from another world. A chicken farmer, Simonton was sitting down to eat when he was shaken by the thundering sound of what he thought was a military plane, flying low overhead. It was not. He raced outside and was confronted by an honest-to-goodness flying saucer, about 30 feet in diameter, hovering above his yard.

Simonton could only stand and stare, in awe, as a doorway opened and a trio of men exited the craft and approached him. They were all short in height—about 5 feet—and wore outfits similar to military jumpsuits. One of the three approached Simonton with what clearly resembled a terrestrial jug, and managed to make Simonton understand that he wanted water. Simonton quickly obliged. As a thank you the aliens gave Simonton a plate of what appeared to be small pancakes. It was a good tradeoff for the farmer. The leader of the group gave a strange salute, and the three returned to the craft and shot away, into the heavens. Simonton ate his pancakes—or, at least, he ate one of them, apparently finding it pretty unappetizing.

There's absolutely no doubt that—just as is the case with the affair of Truman Bethurum—the story of Joe Simonton stretches credulity not just to the limit but, some would surely say, way past it. But, the tale is not quite over. Simonton wasted no time in calling the police— which is, perhaps, an unlikely thing a hoaxer would consider doing. In no time, the U.S. Air Force was in on the action, too—as was the media. Interestingly, the Air Force concluded that Simonton had not concocted the story for money, attention, or infamy, but that he had experienced it in a strange, dream-like state. And there's one other thing, too: I mentioned that Simonton only ate one of the pancakes.

Simonton's decision to preserve the remaining pancakes was a wise one. The Air Force had its scientists analyze one. The result of the analysis demonstrated just one anomaly. The pancake was identical to any other pancake, except for one thing: It was totally lacking in salt.

Two of the main ingredients in pancakes are milk and eggs. A cup of the former contains approximately 100 mg of sodium. It was never explained how, if Simonton was responsible for the whole thing—even if in an altered state, rather than engaging in deception—he had managed to remove the salt from the pancakes, to the point where not even a single molecule of salt could be found. The skeptic might say: So what? Well, it turns out that in fairy lore, the "little people" cannot abide salt. In addition, legend says, if a person scatters salt grains on the ground in front of a fairy, he or she has no choice but to count every single grain—a tedious task, to say the least. So, what we have with the case of Joe Simonton is an encounter with a group of relatively small humanoids who had an aversion to salt. Fairies, aliens, or are they one and the same?

"We Daren't Go A-Hunting, For Fear of Little Men"

It's important to note that Joe Simonton's account is not a standalone one. Walter Yeeling Evans-Wentz was an authority on fairy lore and the author of a still-cherished 1911 book, *The Fairy Faith in Celtic Countries*. He told an intriguing story that somewhat parallels that of Joe Simonton. It revolved around an Irishman, Pat Feeny, who received a strange visit from a diminutive woman asking for oatmeal. Evans-Wentz said: "Paddy had so little that he was ashamed to offer it, so he offered her some potatoes instead, but she wanted oatmeal, and then he gave her all that he had. She told him to place it back in the bin till she should return for it. This he did, and the next morning the bin was overflowing with oatmeal. The woman was one of the Gentry" (Evans-Wentz, 2004).

And also on a similar path, there is the 1850 poem of William Allingham, "The Fairies," in which Allingham referenced "crispy pancakes" as being none other than the food of the fairy folk or, as he called them, "little men." He even made a connection to the curious matter of owls. Allingham's poem begins as follows:

> Up the airy mountain
> Down the rushy glen,
> We daren't go a-hunting,
> For fear of little men;
> Wee folk, good folk,
> Trooping all together;
> Green jacket, red cap,
> And white owl's feather.
> Down along the rocky shore
> Some make their home,
> They live on crispy pancakes
> Of yellow tide-foam;
> Some in the reeds
> Of the black mountain-lake,
> With frogs for their watch-dogs,
> All night awake (Allingham, 1850).

Allingham also describes what sounds like a classic case of alien abduction and missing time:

> They stole little Bridget
> For seven years long;
> When she came down again
> Her friends were all gone.
> They took her lightly back,
> Between the night and morrow,
> They thought that she was fast asleep,
> But she was dead with sorrow.
> They have kept her ever since.
> Deep within the lake,
> On a bed of fig leaves,
> Watching till she wake (Ibid.).

Poet William Allingham.

Extraterrestrials on the Airwaves

Then there are the experiences of a young man named Bob Renaud, which occurred just three months after Joe Simonton's odd encounter. On one particular night in July 1961, Renaud picked up an extraordinary message while "browsing around the shortwave bands" in his small, Massachusetts town (Keel, 2014). It began with a series of bleeps but was soon replaced by a female voice, which later identified herself as Linn-Erri from the planet Korendor.

As was the case in so many Contactee-themed cases of the 1950s and 1960s, Renaud had repeated and extensive chats with his new-found alien friends, many of which were focused on the aliens' fears that we (the human race) were on the verge of destroying ourselves. Also closely following the trend of so many Contactees, Linn-Erri and her comrades took Renaud on trips to secret, alien installations and taught him to create complex machines, one of which was some-what akin to an old-style television set. It reportedly allowed Renaud to see Linn-Erri in the flesh, so to speak. She was a ravishing blond, who looked to be about 19 years of age, but who claimed to be closer to her mid-70s—in human years. A never-aging Anunnaki, perhaps?

It's not unreasonable to suggest that this could all have been provoked by nothing stranger than the late-night, hormone-driven fantasies of a young man run wild. But, as with the equally controversial sagas of Truman Bethurum and Joe Simonton, there is something that makes Bob Renaud's story highly relevant to the book you are now reading. The name Linn-Erri, is very similar to the Gaelic word *Lionmhairreacht*, which is pronounced "Lin-errich" and translates into English as "abundance" (Strieber, 1987).

On top of that, even the name of the aliens' alleged home planet, Korendor, is worth commenting on: It's a word very similar—if not near-identical—to the Gaelic *Cor-Endor*, which means "mound of Endor," or, as Whitley Strieber described it, "a place of oracle" (Ibid.).

From Finland to Flying Saucers

Betty Andreasson is someone who has had a lifetime of profound interaction with otherworld entities. On one occasion in the 1960s, when Andreasson was deep in channeling-style conversation with a small, large-headed alien being named Quaazga, a curious statement was made to Andreasson in a language that she could not understand. One person *did* understand it, however—a man named Leonard Keane. Listening to audio-recordings of Andreasson relating the statement word for word, he concluded the alien was speaking in a form of ancient Gaelic, which translated to the following: "The living descendants of the Northern Peoples are groping in universal darkness. Their mother mourns. A dark occasion forebodes when weakness in high places will revive a high cost of living, an interval of mistakes in high places, an interval fit for distressing events" (Strieber, 1988).

Betty Andreasson had no awareness of the Gaelic tongue. In fact, she was of Finnish-English origin. It turns out, rather notably, that the Finnish people have higher than normal levels of Rh negatives in their midst.

What both this chapter and the preceding one tell us is something of infinite importance: that a study of certain, 20th-century UFO incidents demonstrates connections to the world of the ancient Celts, to people with Y chromosomes that turn out to be, as the University College London noted, indistinguishable from those of the Basque people, and who are clearly Cro-Magnon-like, and to suggestive links to the Anunnaki.

On top of that, Betty Andreasson's associations with Finland, and Antonio Villas Boas's Brazilian connections—two countries with high percentages of Rh negatives—cannot be ignored. Nor can the fact that there are notable cases on record where alien visitations and ancient Celtic terminology go together hand in glove: FirKon, Aura Rhanes, Korendor, and Linn-Erri being just four of many examples. There is also the fact that both the Bethurum and the Villas Boas cases had clear and undeniable sexual and reproductive aspects to them. Certain portions of the Celtic-themed Bob Renaud affair of 1961 simmered with sexual and sensual suggestion, as do Celtic fairy encounters of centuries past.

It's appropriate to close this chapter with the words of Whitley Strieber, who says of the Celtic-Gaelic/UFO connection: "It almost begins to seem as if what we are witnessing now is the discovery of an age-old relationship between ourselves and something that has always been completely misunderstood" (Strieber, 1987).

· The Arrival of the Abductors ·

The accounts of both Truman Bethurum and Antonio Villas Boas were reported quite widely in UFO-themed books, magazines, and newsletters in decades past. It was, however, the overtly sexual nature of the claims that led many researchers of the UFO phenomenon to ignore, or completely write off, the cases as fanciful tales born out of fantasy, wishful thinking, and not a lot else. That situation changed post–September 19, 1961. That was the night when what is widely considered to be a downright historic UFO encounter occurred. It was nowhere near as sexually driven as the Villas Boas case, but it did have an important, human reproductive angle to it. This was something that undeniably set the scene for what followed later—namely, extensive research suggesting that an alien-human breeding program not only existed millennia ago, but *continues* to exist, despite the apparent exit of the Anunnaki, or the vast majority of them, thousands of years ago.

If the Anunnaki *did*, ultimately, leave our world for their ill-fated, degrading home planet, then how, precisely, might just such a program be continued, without their ongoing presence? As noted earlier, there is a distinct possibility the Anunnaki may have left behind them a veritable army of what we might call biological "drones," caretakers created, crafted, and programmed to perform specific tasks—including overseeing a long-term, genetic manipulation of humankind, while their god-like overlords remain absent from view.

The aforementioned date of September 19, 1961—specifically that night—was when a New Hampshire husband and wife, Barney and Betty Hill, were driving to their New Hampshire home after taking a welcome vacation in Montreal, Canada. One might argue they needed another vacation after experiencing what was lurking and looming on the horizon.

Kidnappers From Above

As the pair headed home, and at around 10:30 p.m., as they drove south of Lancaster, New Hampshire, they were puzzled by the sight of a strange light in the night sky above. Viewing the lighted object through binoculars convinced the Hills that what they were seeing was not an aircraft—of either a commercial or military kind. As they continued their drive through the mountains, Barney and Betty developed an uneasy sense that whoever was flying the craft was specifically watching *them*—playing a game with them, toying with them, and practically goading them into following the maneuvers of the mysterious vehicle.

Matters came to a sudden hair-raising head when the object approached their car and dropped to a height of around 90 feet, causing a terrified Barney to bring the car to a sudden stop, in the middle of the road, on the darkened, mountain pass. Pancake-like was how Barney later described the unearthly looking vehicle, after stepping out of the car and staring into the dark skies. As Barney focused on the craft with the binoculars, he couldn't fail to see close to a dozen beings—wearing caps—milling around and peering down at the now deeply frightened pair. When the machine began to close in on the Hills' car, Barney shouted to Betty that the things inside were going to kidnap them. They jumped back into the car at sped off at high speed, which is hardly surprising. Craft and crew did not follow—or so it seemed at the time.

Hypnosis, Buried Memories, and Probing for Pregnancy

The traumatic encounter was far from over. It didn't take long at all before Betty and Barney realized that there was something very wrong about their journey: About two hours of time was missing from it. Gone. Obliterated from their memories. Finally, after nightmares, restless nights of tossing and turning, and picking up on fragmented memories suggesting there was far more to the incident than they consciously remembered, the pair received help from a psychiatrist and neurologist in Boston, Massachusetts, Dr. Benjamin Simon, who began a series of hypnotic sessions with the Hills in January 1964.

What surfaced out of those sessions, while Barney and Betty were rendered into altered states by the doctor, was, to put it bluntly, astounding: If the results of the hypnosis were not the product of fantasy or suggestion, both of the Hills had been taken aboard what was nothing less than an alien spacecraft and subjected to a number of medical procedures that clearly left Betty and Barney in states of lasting turmoil. One of those procedures—specifically performed on Betty—gave an indication that human reproduction somehow played a role in the matter. And something that Barney reported, it will soon be revealed, has a major bearing on the Rh negative issue. The modern era of alien abductions, and that attendant matter of a connection to human reproduction and an alien bloodline, was about to be born.

The story is a remarkable one, and one that is comprised of Betty's and Barney's own memories that flooded back into their mind during distressing dreams as well as data that surfaced during the hypnosis sessions with Dr. Simon. We'll start with Betty. According to Betty, while under the control and sway of the strange creatures that stood before her on the craft, she experienced something deeply traumatic: Laid out flat on something similar to an operating table, Betty—to her horror—witnessed one of the entities inserting a needle-like device into her navel, after informing her he was going to check if she was pregnant. In addition, Betty said the alien performing the procedure assured her that the test would be very helpful—but in what way, and why, exactly, were not explained. Nor was it explained who the procedure would be helpful for: Betty or the ETs. One suspects the latter.

According to Betty, the needle was somewhere between 4 and 6 inches in length and had a tube attached to it. Far from feeling like the slight discomfort associated with a regular medical needle, however, Betty said that the pain—as it was inserted—was more along the lines of what she thought it would feel like to have the blade of a knife plunged into her. In other words, it was *excruciating*. Both the entity carrying out the task, and an additional one that was perceived by the Hills as the leader, reacted in a surprised and concerned fashion—to the extent that the creature overseeing the situation waved his hand across Betty's eyes, something that immediately removed all of the agony. At least, that was the scenario in Betty's dreams.

Under hypnosis, however, the story was that the pain did not go away: Betty was still in pain and deeply stressed. This is highly suggestive of the probability that her subconscious state had attempted to place a more positive, and far less traumatic, slant on the experience—but one that the hypnosis sessions demonstrated was far worse than her mind was trying to telling her. In fact, such was the stressful, pain-filled, and fear-dominated state that Betty was in, Dr. Simon took the immediate step of bringing the hypnotic session to a rapid halt. This particular aspect of the Hill affair brings us to the matter of something called amniocentesis.

An Alien Equivalent of Amniocentesis?

When a woman becomes pregnant, the developing fetus is enveloped in what is termed amniotic fluid. It is a liquid that is very much like water, and from a study of which a great deal can be ascertained about the health and development of the fetus. Alpha-fetoprotein and developing skin cells are two of the main things that the amniocentesis procedure focuses on, as it seeks to confirm the condition of the fetus.

During the process, a needle is inserted into the mother's uterus, via her abdomen, usually between 15 and 18 weeks into pregnancy. Because the procedure can at times be a tricky one, it is constantly overseen via ultrasound scanning. The goal is to use the needle to secure a small amount of amniotic fluid, which can then be studied and analyzed. Typically, the procedure is performed for genetic reasons, such as to determine if the developing baby may have muscular dystrophy, cystic fibrosis, or Down syndrome. It's a procedure which is very often undertaken on women in their mid-30s or older (and who have a markedly higher chance of developing chromosomal disorders), and those who have given birth to a previous child with either physical or mental disorders. It may not be a coincidence that when Betty was subjected to that curious procedure, she was already in her early 40s.

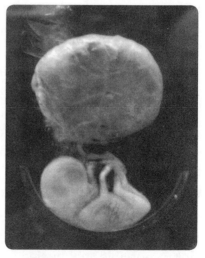

Rather notably, one of the risks associated with amniocentesis is directly connected to the matter of the Rh negatives. During the process of utilizing a needle to secure skin cells and alpha-fetoprotein from the fetus, blood cells from the baby may enter the bloodstream of the mother. If mother and baby have the same blood, there is no problem. If, however, the mother is Rh negative and the child is not, Rh sensitization will occur and the mother's body will immediately begin creating antibodies to attack the fetus's blood cells. Only by giving the mother

The unborn human fetus.

the drug Rh immunoglobulin can the baby be free of attack from its very own parent.

A mniocentesis or Something Else?

It must be said that there is one notable difference between amniocentesis and the procedure that Betty Hill experienced—namely, that the needle inserted into Betty went via her navel. In amniocentesis, it's via the abdomen and then into the uterus. Nevertheless, it's still astonishing that Betty's aliens informed her that the needle-inserting procedure was linked with determining if she was pregnant.

Those doubtful of Betty's account might take note of the fact that in 1930, the team of Leland E. Holly, Thomas Orville Menees, and J. Duane Miller, performed an amniocentesis procedure on a pregnant woman. In this case, it involved injecting dye into the amniotic sac, specifically to study the placenta and the fetus. It was also used, as far back as the 1950s, to determine if an Rh negative woman was carrying an Rh positive baby. It was, however, a procedure that remained extremely dicey until the early 1970s, when the introduction of ultrasound technology was applied to the process of securing alpha-fetoprotein and skin cells.

Could Betty have heard of, or read about, these early, pre-1960s era examples of amniocentesis? Certainly, it's not impossible. In addition, in 1960, only one year before the encounter of the Hills, and for the very first time, amniocentesis was used to identify hemophilia-related issues relative to mother and fetus. It was a development reported on, at the time—though primarily in the pages of in-house medical journals, of a type that Betty was unlikely to have come across. If Betty did have an awareness of what amniocentesis is, it's not impossible that buried memories of reading about it had a bearing on both her dream-based and hypnotic recollections. But, on the other hand, why would Betty say the needle was inserted into her navel, if she knew that amniocentesis was a technique that was focused only on the abdomen and the uterus?

In some respects, what Betty told of sounds far more like a laparoscopy, in which a small insertion is made into the belly and a lighted tube is inserted to allow for an examination of the pelvic organs to be undertaken. Given that the pelvic organs include the uterus, the fallopian tubes, the vagina, and the ovaries, a solid case can *still* be made that the procedure performed on Betty was specifically of a gynecological nature, even if it wasn't a case of amniocentesis.

The Strange Story of Barney's Spine

Having addressed one of the most significant procedures performed on Betty Hill, let's take a look at two experiences reported by her husband, Barney, both of which have a bearing on the overall story that this book tells. At one point, while Barney was being medically examined, one of the entities placed something over his penis that caused him to orgasm and ejaculate. The inference is that the aliens wished to obtain a sample of Barney's sperm. There then followed a much stranger procedure: One of the creatures carefully ran its fingers down the entire length of Barney's spine. So carefully and precisely was the action taken, Barney came to suspect the alien was counting how many vertebrae Barney had. This might sound odd, at first glance. Upon taking a second look, however, there may have been a very good reason for performing a task that many might find downright peculiar or even unnecessary.

About one in 10 of the world's population is born with an extra, sixth lumbar vertebra. What is particularly interesting, however, is that the percentage of Rh negatives with an additional vertebra is significant. With this in mind, one could make a logical assumption that the alien in question was trying to determine if Barney was Rh negative.

It's also worth noting that although most people associate the experience of the Hills with the so-called, diminutive, skinny, hairless, large-headed, and black-eyed Grays of alien abduction lore, the fact is that Betty described the entities as having dark hair, pronounced foreheads, and large noses that reminded her of the nose of Jimmy Durante. For those who are not aware of who Durante was, he was an Italian-American comedian noted for his huge nose. Interestingly, a careful look at Durante's nose reveals it was not at all dissimilar to that of the Neanderthals, who are part and parcel of the Rh negative controversy. The pronounced foreheads as described by Betty were also typical of the Neanderthals, as, almost certainly, was the dark hair she described them as having. Should we consider that the aliens encountered by Barney and Betty Hill, late one night in September 1961, had a lineage extending back to the days of the Cro-Magnons, the Neanderthals, and the DNA-manipulating Anunnaki? Maybe, yes.

Barney Hill died in 1969; he was only 46 years of age. Betty lived on until 2004, when she passed on at the ripe old age of 85. As a result, many aspects of the Hill case elude us and are likely to continue to do so. It should, however, be kept firmly in mind that (1) a procedure was performed on Betty that was not unlike amniocentesis (which, as we have seen, can have a bearing on issues concerning an Rh negative, pregnant woman carrying an Rh positive fetus); and (2) steps were taken to count Barney's lumbar vertebra, something that may well be related to the matter of many Rh negatives having an extra vertebra.

Many investigators of the UFO phenomenon perceive the Hill case as one of the most important cases on record—from a historical perspective and from the angle of it being the first, high-profile example of alien abduction. The incident may also be significant from the undeniable, but until now largely unappreciated, connection to the domain of the Rh negatives.

14

· The Abduction Epidemic Begins ·

If the September 1961 incident reported by Barney and Betty Hill had been a one-off, singular event, then there might be at least *some* justification in suggesting that the whole event was born out of some strange, shared psychological event. It was *not* a singular event, however. Quite the contrary, it was just the start of a veritable deluge of reports that continues to this very day. Somewhat curiously, although abductions increased post-1961, in the immediate years after the experience of the Hills, the sexual and reproduction aspects were very much few and far between. Take, for example, the case of one Herbert Schirmer.

In the early hours of December 3, 1967, Schirmer—a policeman in Ashland, Nebraska—was driving around town, checking that all was normal. It turns out that things were *not* normal; they were *far* from being normal. As he scoured the deserted, quiet streets, Schirmer was suddenly confronted by what, at first glance, he thought was a broken-down truck at the edge of one particular road. When his headlights hit the object with full force, however, it became instantly clear to Schirmer that this was no truck.

What Schirmer was confronted by was a fairly compact, egg-shaped vehicle, floating around 8 to 10 feet above the surface of the road. An amazed Schirmer could only stare with amazement as the UFO—there was really no other way to describe it—rose further into the sky, amid a flashing of red lights and a wailing, banshee-like sound, and then exited the area by taking a course directly above Schirmer's vehicle. He sat there, amazed, for a few moments, and then quickly headed back to the police station. He feverishly recorded the details in the logbook: "Saw a flying saucer at the junction of highways 6 and 63. Believe it or not!" (Blum and Blum, 1978).

Just like Betty and Barney Hill, Schirmer very soon came to realize that certain portions of that strange night were gone from his mind and memory—specifically, an hour or so of time. Also paralleling the Hills' experience, Schirmer elected to undergo hypnosis to try to figure out what on earth (or off of it) had occurred. The hypnotic sessions were carried out by a Boulder, Colorado–based Dr. Leo Sprinkle. While under hypnosis, Schirmer provided an incredible account of what happened during that absent period of time.

Taken Aboard a UFO

As he sat in his police car, staring in awe at the hovering craft directly before him, Schirmer was confronted by three beings, all wearing tight-fitting, one-piece outfits, that exited the craft and walked toward him. All were around 4 1/2 to 5 feet in height. Approaching the driver's side window, one—which Schirmer perceived to be the "leader" of the alien pack—leaned in, in a slightly menacing fashion, and asked, "Are you the watchman of this place?" Schirmer replied that, yes, he was. As the aliens stood around his squad car, Schirmer couldn't fail to notice that their uniforms displayed, rather intriguingly, the image of a winged serpent. The matter of winged serpents is highly significant to the saga of the Aztec and Toltec god Quetzalcoatl (related in a later chapter of this book), who may very well have been one of the legendary Anunnaki (Ibid.).

Quetzalcoatl, the serpent god.

Schirmer was reportedly taken aboard the craft, given what we would call a tour, and told, in somewhat puzzling and enigmatic words, by the head alien: "We want you to believe in us, but not too much." After this, he was returned to his vehicle, with his mind wiped clean of the events—until definitively bad dreams forced him to undergo hypnosis, and the startling saga came tumbling out in spectacular fashion (Ibid.).

Kidnapped From the Pascagoula River

Moving on to 1973—specifically the night of October 10th— there is the fantastic report of Calvin Parker and Charles Hickson, who, on the night at issue, were having a fine, relaxing time fishing on the banks of the Pascagoula River, Mississippi. It was roughly 9 p.m. when the attention of both men was caught by a curious light coming across the waters of the river and in their very direction. As the light closed in, Hickson and Parker could see it for what it really was: an oval-shaped vehicle that gave off a slight, nausea-inducing hum and an array of dazzling, bright lights. Suddenly, a hatch opened in the side of the craft and three figures—all vaguely human in shape, but gray in color, with lobster-like claws, and faces that appeared somewhat masked and displaying carrot-like protrusions— emerged. They glided eerily and silently, across and above the river, right toward the petrified pair.

Whether it was due to some unearthly power of the terrifying trio from the stars, or just pure, cold fear on the part of Hickson and Parker, neither man was able to move a muscle. They were like the proverbial deer caught in the proverbial headlights. The creatures lunged for both men, who were quickly taken aboard the craft. Hickson's book explains that according to Parker, as he lay on some kind of table, a female entity inserted a needle into the base of his penis—shades, of course, of Betty Hill's story of her aliens inserting a needle into her navel. When the procedure was over, both men— groggy and unsure what had just happened—were unceremoniously deposited back on the edge of the river, from where they had originally been taken. It was an incident that led Parker to retreat into a world of anonymity, and Hickson to write a book on the affair and become a celebrity on the UFO lecture circuit.

Trauma in the Woods

Two years after the Hickson-Parker incident, on the night of November 5, 1975, it was the turn of a man named Travis Walton to be kidnapped, in traumatic fashion, from a logging site in the Apache-Sigreaves National Forest, in Arizona. As terrified colleagues looked on, Walton was hit by a bright light that emanated from a significantly sized, gold-colored UFO that had caught the group's attention and that Walton had raced toward. His friends fled the scene when Walton was hit by the beam and, incredibly, rose slightly off the ground. Walton was neither seen nor heard from for another five days.

On his return, Walton told a story that was as fantastic as it was controversial. Like so many other alien abductees, Walton's next recollection, after the cosmic confrontation in the woods, was of waking up on a bed-like structure, around which was a trio of small figures, with large heads and piercing eyes. There followed a near-violent confrontation between Walton and the three, an encounter with a being that looked practically human, and an experience with a female alien who placed something over Walton's mouth and face that most closely resembled a gas mask. After that, there was nothing—at least, not until he awoke, groggy and confused, in the town of Heber, Arizona. Decades later, the story of Travis Walton continues to be debated amid those places where Ufologists gather.

•••

That, in essence, is a summary of several of the most prominent alien abduction cases that occurred in both the immediate- and long-term wake of the Betty and Barney Hill incident of September 1961. Of those cases, the only one with a semblance of a sexual/reproductive component attached to it was that of Calvin Parker. As the 1970s gave way to the 1980s, however, there was a dramatic and sudden shift and increase in the number of alien abductions reported, and particularly so across the United States—nearly all of which were dominated by matters relative to eggs, sperm, gene-splicing, and the birth of what have become known as alien-human hybrids.

15

· Missing Time ·

The person who largely and almost singlehandedly kick-started the next aspect of this story of genetic manipulation of the human race by advanced extraterrestrials was a Virginia-born painter named Budd Hopkins. It was Hopkins's 1981 book, *Missing Time*, that really set the cat among the pigeons, as we shall now see. The abduction stories of Betty and Barney Hill, Travis Walton, Herbert Schirmer, and Charles Hickson and Calvin Parker were undeniably fascinating, and they most assuredly made the UFO research community sit up and take notice of something astounding: People were being kidnapped and subjected to intrusive and frightening medical procedures by creatures from other worlds. There is, however, an important issue that needs to be stressed, and that demonstrates how and why the sheer scale of the alien abduction phenomenon remained under-appreciated until Hopkins was on the scene.

The Hill case occurred in 1961. Herbert Schirmer was taken on board a UFO in 1967. Hickson and Parker's abduction was in 1973. And Travis Walton was taken in 1975. That's just four cases across 14 years. Yes, there were other, less-well-profiled, abductions throughout that time period, but the image that these incidents provoked was one that suggested abductions were things that occurred only now and again. It was not a case of aliens routinely abducting people on a regular basis, all across the planet. Well, actually *it was*. It was Hopkins, whose abduction research began in 1976, that we have to thank for demonstrating that what appeared to be a few, random events was actually nothing of the sort. It was a downright *epidemic*.

Tagging, Tracking, and "Taking Something"

More disturbing, Hopkins's work showed that, in many cases, abductions did not begin when people matured and were adults. They commenced in the formative years of childhood and very often ran through numerous generations of the same families. In some cases, Hopkins found, people were being implanted with small devices—for purposes that no-one could ascertain. Maybe they were designed to tag people, allowing the ETs to track the abductees throughout their lives, no matter where they might relocate to on the planet. A far more sinister theory suggested that the implants were designed to do nothing less than alter the behavior of the abductees. In no time at all, the somewhat-innocent days of Betty and Barney Hill were overthrown by fears of alien-orchestrated Manchurian Candidates and hypnotically controlled abductees.

Budd Hopkins, author of Missing Time.

Hopkins's early work, as published in *Missing Time* in 1981, also sowed the seeds for something else: a deep and nagging suspicion that part of the alien abduction agenda—and, just perhaps, *all* of it—was based around matters of a reproductive, genetic nature. Hopkins asked of this issue: "What if the UFO occupants are *taking* something from their captives?" (Hopkins, 1981).

He answered his own question with the following words: "We may indeed possess something—a natural resource, an element, a genetic structure—that an alien culture might desire to use, for example, as raw material" (Ibid.).

Hopkins may well have been right on target with his references to a "genetic structure" and "raw material," both of which hark back to the days of the Anunnaki and their widespread alteration of the human species. Hopkins's book proved to be a major talking point within the field of Ufology and firmly set the scene for what was to follow (Ibid.).

Intruders and *Communion*

Budd Hopkins continued to intensively investigate alien abduction claims in the 1980s, and to the extent that a clear pattern of DNA fingerprinting, the extraction of ova and sperm from abductees, and suspicions of a massive, alien-driven operation to use the human race in some huge, genetics-driven program, took firm shape. In 1987, matters really came to a head: Hopkins's follow-up book, *Intruders*, was published, which told the story of alien abductee Kathie Davies. It was a book that reinforced the scenarios detailed in *Missing Time*. By far the most important development in the alien abduction phenomenon in 1987, however, was the publication of Whitley Strieber's huge best-seller *Communion*.

Strieber, previously known for such horror-fiction novels as *The Wolfen* and *The Hunger*, told an incredible story of a traumatic December 1985 experience of definitive alien abduction proportions. Not only that, Strieber's book was quite unlike anything else that had, up until that point, ever been published on the abduction controversy. Yes, *Communion* demonstrated that Strieber had undergone something that fitted the abduction template. But, he also veered off into territories that few UFO researchers had previously negotiated.

In researching his own experiences, Strieber came across data that demonstrated a connection between the names and language of certain alien entities and the Celtic people of times long gone—as noted in a previous chapter. Strieber also began to dig deep into ancient fairy lore, noting for his readers the undeniable parallels between encounters with the little people and today's Grays, and with the missing time angle being one of the most visible and obvious of all the parallels. He also delved deep into the curious connection between alien encounters and owls—the latter being a staple part of the lore surrounding the Anunnaki Lilith. At the time, however, many within Ufology, galvanized by the words of Hopkins, wanted to hear solely about implants, spaceships, and creatures from other planets engaging in bizarre experiments on targeted people.

Yes, *Communion* covered all those points that so excited and enthused the UFO research community. But, Strieber was astute enough to realize that even if that was exactly what was taking place, it did not tell the *entire* story. What Strieber did in his book was to demonstrate—in a soundly argued fashion—that the alien abduction phenomenon is not a recent one. It did not begin with Betty and Barney Hill, or even with Antonio Villas Boas. It was as old as us, the human race, and probably much older—*infinitely* older.

Strieber's 1988 follow-up book, *Transformation*, added to the controversy, as did subsequent titles, such as *The Secret School* and *Breakthrough*. Strieber's collective work did something else, too: It caught the attention of the mainstream media. After all, how could it not: *Communion* hit the number-one spot on the *New York Times* best-seller list. By the end of the 1980s, and as a new decade loomed large, tales of alien abductions, and matters relative to stolen sperm, purloined ova, and strange devices buried under people's skin, were *everywhere*.

A Harvard Professor Gets on the Trail of the Abductors

The 1990s saw the alien abduction phenomenon reach positively stratospheric proportions. Much of this was a result of the work of two men: John E. Mack, MD, and David M. Jacobs, PhD. It must be said, however, that they brought very different concepts and thoughts to the table. Mack, a Pulitzer Prize–winning author (of a book on T.E. Lawrence, better known as Lawrence of Arabia) who was killed in 2004, in London, England, by a drunk driver, penned two books that left a big mark on 1990s-era Ufology: *Abduction* and *Passport to the Cosmos.* Certainly, one of the chief reasons why Mack's books became such talking points wasn't just because of their subject matter. It was because Mack was a Harvard Medical School professor—and he was talking about alien abductions from the perspective of them being all too shockingly real. Needless to say, none of this went down well with the bigwigs at Harvard, and in May 1994 Mack's work in the field of alien abductions came under rapid, unrelenting fire. The result: Daniel C. Tosteson, who was the dean of the Harvard Medical School, set up a group to carefully assess the nature of clinical care given by Mack to his growing body of abductees. The conclusions of the group were damning.

Mack's attorney, Daniel Sheehan, said that Tosteson's group concluded that it was

> professionally irresponsible for any academic, scholar or practicing psychiatrist to give any credence whatsoever to any personal report of a direct personal contact between a human being and an Extraterrestrial Being until after the person has been subjected to every possible available battery of standard psychological tests which might conceivably explain the report as the product of some known form of clinical psychosis. To communicate, in any way whatsoever, to a person who has reported a "close encounter" with an Extraterrestrial life form that this experience might well have been realis professionally irresponsible (Klass, 1995).

Nevertheless, Mack retained his standing at Harvard and continued his abduction-based work until the time of his death in London. Where Mack differed from so many other UFO researchers that were studying the phenomenon was from the perspective of the spiritual nature of certain abduction events. Mack held the view that there was a *deep* spiritual aspect to the mystery and that people were transformed—in a positive fashion—by their experiences. He noted, for example, that post-abduction they often developed concerns about the environment. They pondered the matter of life after death, karma and fate, and the nature of the human soul, and they underwent out-of-body experiences and near-death events—from which they came back positively transformed.

Mack said: "The abduction phenomenon seems to me to be a part of the shift in consciousness that is collapsing duality and enabling us to see that we are connected beyond the Earth at a cosmic level" (Mack, 1999).

And then there was Professor David M. Jacobs.

Creating Something That *Looks* Human—But *Isn't*

Before we get to the matter of Jacobs, it is both important and relevant to note that the 1990s was also the decade in which another aspect of alien abduction lore reached its absolute pinnacle. It was the matter of what have become known as alien-human hybrids. Certainly, both the Antonio Villas Boas case of 1957 and the Betty and Barney Hill encounter of 1961 strongly suggested there was what we might call a "reproductive component" to abductions. Budd Hopkins's work, showing that ova and sperm were being taken from kidnapped Americans, reinforced that particular theory even more. All of that, however, was overshadowed by the rise of the hybrids.

As the 1990s progressed, controversial, and even frightening, accounts surfaced of alien abductees encountering—usually onboard UFOs—young children that gave every appearance of being half-human and half-alien, and specifically of the Gray type. They *looked* human, but there were certain things that *were just not right*. Their skin was pale, almost to the point of appearing anemic. Their limbs were thin, bony, and fragile-looking. Their eyes were overly large, and noticeably oval- or almond-shaped, exactly like those of the Grays. Their hair was thin and wispy. And it wasn't just hybrid children that abductees reported encountering: It was hybrid *fetuses*, too. In many such cases, witnesses claimed to have seen such fetuses being *grown*—in huge, glass tanks filled with milky liquid.

The implication was, for some, terrifying: Aliens, from who knew where, were creating and refining creatures that resembled us (providing one did not get *too* close a look at them), that could pass for us, that could move among us, and that might even have an agenda of *infiltrating* us. And yes, I *do* mean that from a sinister, and potentially hostile, perspective. There is something else too: The hybrids were the undeniable modern-day equivalents of the so-called changelings of centuries-old Celtic lore concerning fairies—things created by the wee folk and that were designed to replace babies snatched in the night and whisked away to the domain of the fairies—who, as we have seen, may actually have been creations of the Anunnaki. All of this brings us to Professor Jacobs.

The Threat

Budd Hopkins was of the opinion that, even if the Grays *were* exploiting people and taking their DNA, sperm, and eggs, and all against their will, the alien abduction phenomenon was still, essentially, a benign one. John Mack considered the abduction experience to be downright positive and spiritually uplifting, even. Professor Jacobs, however, had a very different line of thought—and he still does. The author of, among other titles, *The Threat: Revealing the Secret Alien Agenda*, Jacobs makes no bones about his beliefs. He strongly suspects that the creation of what we might call an underground, alien army is well underway—that something from somewhere else is clandestinely working its way into human civilization, its numbers rising and its intentions bleak. For us, at least. Not for them, of course.

Jacobs says: "Many people think that abductions are a 'study' or 'experiment,' or that the aliens are 'learning' about us. The numbers suggest otherwise. The learning and experimenting, of ever the case, are mainly over. Hence, the evidence clearly indicates that the aliens are conducting a widespread, systematic *program of physiological exploitation* of human beings" (emphasis added) (Jacobs, 1999).

In the next couple of chapters, let's take a much closer look at the possibly ominous entities that may be among us. Their names include not just the hybrids, but also, and most ominous of all, the Black-Eyed Children.

Children of the Gods

Reports of so-called hybrid children and hybrid babies are particularly notable, in the sense that encounters with these somewhat-unsettling creatures more often than not follow certain, distinct pathways that crop up time and again. There is, for example, most assuredly a greater percentage of female abductees who have had interactions with the hybrids than there are male abductees. There appears to be a very good reason for this.

Under hypnotic regression, numerous women have reported being taken aboard a UFO or, on more than a few occasions, to an underground installation, where they are introduced to the hybrids. Of course, the underground component parallels the centuries-old fairy encounters and the changeling phenomenon, as discussed in an earlier chapter. In such situations the woman will either be laying on something akin to an operating-room table, or sitting in a chair that resembles a dentist's chair. It's then that something remarkable happens—although, admittedly, others might call it utterly terrifying.

The World of the Hybrids

As the abductee looks on, a group of three or four Grays will approach, with one of them holding in their hands a tiny baby that is clearly not entirely human, even though it exhibits certain physical, human traits. The abductee is then encouraged to take the baby from the Gray and to cradle it. Researchers of the phenomenon have suggested, probably correctly, that this procedure is undertaken to try to instill an emotional bond between the abductee and the hybrid. If this all sounds very calm and tranquil, it very often is the precise opposite.

Many of the female abductees who report this bonding process— or *attempt* at bonding—were, months earlier, pregnant themselves. For a while, at least, they were. There are many reports on record where a pregnant abductee has experienced a sudden, unexplained miscarriage—a tragic event, to be sure. Or is there just an assumption they were miscarriages? Quite possibly, yes.

Those same abductees, when presented with a hybrid baby, develop sudden, unexplained suspicions that what they are being shown is the baby they were once carrying and that they assumed had miscarried. In this scenario, abduction researchers suggest, the abductees are impregnated during an earlier abduction, they then carry the fetus for a number of months, and then it is removed from the mother during a later abduction and essentially "grown" in what we might call an artificial womb. A sensational—some might say outrageous—scenario, to be sure, but it's not a possibility that can be dismissed. The reason why it is as amazing as it is controversial: We, the human race, are now working—and working hard and fast—to develop artificial wombs.

Giving Birth Without Actually Giving Birth

The process of growing a fetus, and bringing it to full term in an artificial womb, is called ectogenesis. Much of the research is still at a theoretical stage, predominantly because of moral-based restrictions and regulations that govern the ethical, or non-ethical, use of human embryos in experimentation. But, not all of the work is theoretical. As just two perfect examples, we have to first turn our attentions to Japan and experimentation undertaken in 1997 at the

Bunkyo, Tokyo-based Juntendo University. The program was led by Yoshinori Kuwabara, the chairman of the department of obstetrics at the university, who was successful in growing goat embryos that were contained in a machine filled with amniotic fluid, a yellow-colored liquid contained in the amniotic sac and that surrounds the growing fetus. Then there is the work of Cornell University's Reproductive Endocrine Laboratory. In both 2003 and 2011 significant success was had by sustaining embryos in artificial wombs. In the 2003 experiment, the embryo was that of a mouse. Eight years later, however, it was nothing less than a human embryo, which was allowed to develop for 10 days—with 14 days being the absolute, legal time limit on experimenting with human fetuses.

Zoltan Istvan, the founder of the Transhumanist Party, says of a theoretical future in which human babies are no longer birthed but grown—almost in conveyor-belt-style:

> The theory is that every heartbeat, kick, and moment of a fetus's life could be carefully monitored, from zygote to the moment the baby takes its first breath of air. Every nutrient the fetus gets would be measured, every movement it makes would be filmed, every heartbeat would be analyzed for proper timing. As with all new technology, traditional biological and social customs could give way to newer practices promising safety, efficiency, and practicality (Mejia, 2014).

In that sense, the process of effectively leaving the mother out of the equation, and having the nine-month-long process of development handled in an artificial womb, may offer notable advantages. There is, however, one potential disadvantage, and it may prove to be a big one, should we, as a species, ever decide to go down this cold, emotionless pathway. It is the matter of the deep bonding between the mother and the unborn fetus that quickly develops when pregnancy begins—or, in the future, what might very well be a distinct *lack* of that bonding.

Might we see a 23rd century, or a 28th century, in which, as a result of a factory-like environment in which babies are created to order, specification, and design, that bond is completely lost? Might we see the human race, hundreds of years from now, reduced to nothing but cold, emotionless entities—in fact, just like the Grays, rather ironically—that will have no understanding of, or even any care for, the emotional angle of what it means to be pregnant? Such a thing, given that research in this field is pressing ahead, is not at all out of the question. It may be sadly inevitable. This same situation may also explain why the Grays are forced to present hybrid children to human mothers, in an effort to induce bonding: The Grays are utterly incapable of comprehending how to make that bond themselves.

And on this very matter, we have reports from abductees that are downright eerie, in terms of their descriptions of what appear to be artificial wombs aboard UFOs and in below-ground facilities. Professor David Jacobs provides data that is undeniably chilling and that is based on his firsthand work with many victims of alien abduction and genetic manipulation: "Abductees have reported rooms, some small and some almost cavernous, containing hundreds, and even thousands, of tanks with gestating fetuses—their large, open black eyes dominating their tiny bodies. The tanks are often arrayed in gestational stages of development, from youngest to oldest" (Jacobs, 1999).

Jacobs says of one abductee he worked with, Alison, that: "A gray alien told Alison that late-stage fetuses are kept longer in utero because they cannot be sustained in incubators for a long time. Early-stage hybrids, he said, can be kept in the incubators for more sustained periods" (Ibid.).

Then there was the late Dr. Roger Leir, who took things to an even more controversial level with his conclusions that some abductees—particularly those who were part of the hybridization process—were being implanted with infinitely small devices that could track their every single move. Leir's website, Alien Scalpel, states of Leir's work that he and his surgical team have performed fifteen surgeries on alleged alien abductees. This resulted in the removal of sixteen separate and distinct objects suspected of being alien implants. These objects have been scientifically investigated by some of the most prestigious laboratories in the world including Los Alamos National Labs, New Mexico Tech, Seal Laboratories, Southwest Labs, the University of Toronto, York University, and the University of California at San Diego. Their findings have been baffling and some comparisons have been made to Meteorite Samples. In addition some of the tests show metallurgical anomalies such as highly Magnetic Iron that is without crystalline form, combinations of crystalline materials mixed common metals, growth of biological tissue into or out of metallic substances, as well as isotopic ratios not of this world ("Dr. Leir's Bio," 2010).

"Alien implant" authority, the late Roger Leir.

Children That Are Not What They Seem to Be

It should be noted that it's not always just hybrid *babies* that are shown to abductees and with whom they are encouraged to bond. It's very often hybrid *children*, too. As bizarre as it may sound (or, just perhaps, it's not quite so bizarre, after all) abductees report being taken to rooms that are in stark contrast to the sterile and clean—almost obsessively so—environments aboard UFOs. In these particular cases, abductees enter an environment in which hybrid children are given toys to play with—as if a concerted attempt is being made to humanize the hybrids even more. Whether this is done from a positive perspective of inter-species cooperation and inter-breeding, or if it's done to ensure that the hybrids can more successfully infiltrate human society in a sinister, hostile fashion, very much remains to be seen and is dependent on which side of the fence you stand.

Take, for example, the story of Jennifer, a life-long resident of New Jersey. Now 32, she has conscious recall of encounters with the Grays going back to her early childhood, as does her mother. Even her grandmother has vague recollections of encountering a group of "little men" in New Jersey woods, during the summer months, at some point in the 1940s—again, emphasizing the ongoing, multi-generational aspect of these events. As well as her consciously recalled interactions with the Grays, Jennifer has been able to pull further recollections out of the depths of her mind and subconscious via hypnosis. One recollection in particular stands out, in terms of relevancy.

Although Jennifer has no memories of interactions with hybrid babies, she does have memories of being taken, in 2009, to what she described as looking like "an old military base, but shut down," where she encountered hybrid children. (As we will see in a future chapter, there are other examples of abandoned, official facilities seemingly being used in covert abduction-related situations.) Jennifer's hypnotically recovered recollections begin with her stepping out of what she first thought was a large, black sedan, but that, with hindsight, she came to believe was a landed UFO—the image of the car, then, being a screen memory designed to mask, or at least confuse, the true nature of the event. She then recalls being guided, in a somewhat groggy and hazy state, to an elevator by three dwarf-ish figures of which she found difficult to recall, in terms of their physical appearances. What she had no trouble remembering, how-ever, was what happened next (Redfern, interview, 2011).

After what she perceived as an incredibly long descent in the elevator, Jennifer was taken to a large room that was filled with two things: a group of five or six hybrid children, all but one female; and a multitude of toys. Strewn across the floor were teddy bears, dolls, and a large amount of fluffy toy dogs. The hybrids—skinny, sickly looking, yellow-haired, and seemingly disinterested in the toys—were sitting on chairs placed in a row against one of the walls.

It was Jennifer's "job"—as she worded it—to try to encourage the children to play with the toys, something she was only partially successful in doing. Two of them actually smiled and even laughed when Jennifer gently tossed teddy bears in their direction. The others offered little more than disinterest. Time and again, Jennifer was urged to interact with the hybrids. And on each occasion, the response was far from encouraging. Evidently, Jennifer's abductors realized that things were not proceeding well and she was finally motioned to the door. Once again, her mind was filled with images of sitting in a black sedan, and being driven back to her home. Yet, as with her arrival at the facility, she had deep suspicions that the car imagery was, effectively, "implanted" in her mind and did not tell the true story of how she found herself deep underground (Ibid.).

Jennifer's encounter is of a type that many abductees—particularly so for female abductees—have reported. Although we can hope that the attempts of the Grays to have the hybrids interact with the human race has a positive goal in mind, we should still remain mindful of the conclusions of Professor David Jacobs—namely that what is afoot is a subtle, secret, and sinister program of genetic manipulation, designed to allow for the infiltration the human race—infiltration that will ultimately lead to nothing less than full-blown *control*. And from that point onward? Well, the news may be far from good. Are there indications that the hybrids are up to no good? Yes, there certainly are. They are indications that can be found in what is, without doubt, the creepiest development in this ever-expanding saga: the rise of the most terrifying hybrids of all.

17

The Black-Eyed Children

In 1957, an acclaimed British sci-fi writer, John Wyndham (probably best known for his 1951 book, *The Day of the Triffids*), penned a novel titled *The Midwich Cuckoos*. In 1960, it was turned into a hit movie called *Village of the Damned*, which spawned a 1963 sequel, *Children of the Damned*. The story is one that, in a fictional format, has deep parallels to the real world of UFOs and matters that are highly relevant to the hybrids. In Wyndham's story, on one particular morning, all of the residents of the small English village of Midwich are briefly and inexplicably rendered unconscious. They wake soon after, groggy and confused. Indeed, one can convincingly argue they experienced nothing less than alien abduction–style missing time. All seems normal afterward, despite the utterly baffling nature of the village-wide event. As the tale progresses, however, we learn that things are nowhere near normal.

Each and every woman in the village who is capable of giving birth soon finds herself inexplicably pregnant. The pregnancies are not what one would normally expect, however: The fetuses develop at an alarmingly and inexplicably rapid rate. The women all give birth within hours of each other. The babies grow at incredibly fast speeds, taking on the appearance of 7- or 8-year-olds when they are barely actually 3. They are eerily emotionless, have vacant expressions and pale skin, possess eyes that are dominated by jet-black irises, and have the ability to take control of the human mind, in hypnotic-like fashion. Hardly surprisingly, the British government takes a concerned interest, particularly so because similar odd births have been reported in other parts of the world.

As the children continue to grow, so do their intellects and their extraordinary psychic powers—to the extent that the adults soon become the slaves, and, eventually, the all-too-dead victims of the creepy kids. As a result, the race is on to wipe out these possibly half-human/half-alien things (although we are never told this is what they are, the inference is certainly apparent) before they and the others of their kind—specifically in Russia, Canada, and Australia—can exert their murderous tendencies on just about anyone and everyone else.

Both *The Midwich Cuckoos* and the movie adaptation, *The Village of the Damned*, are made all the more extraordinary and thought-provoking as a result of something undeniably astounding: In the late 1990s, a phenomenon began to slowly surface that suggested John Wyndham's novel may not have been mere fiction after all. The homicidal children of Midwich finally had their real-life equivalents. They have become known as the Black-Eyed Children.

It's interesting to note that during the Second World War, Wyndham worked for the British government's Ministry of Information (MoI), whose work was focused on disseminating propaganda to try and affect the moral of the Nazis and also on keeping from the general public certain, sensitive things that the government of the day preferred the rest of us didn't know about. Wyndham retained contacts and friendships with certain senior people from the MoI well into the 1960s. One has to wonder if any of the novel storylines in his books, including *The Midwich Cuckoos*, were based on secrets of a UFO-themed nature that were provided to him by those same contacts. Admittedly, such a possibility remains just a theory, but consider all of the following, and then take note of how closely the phenomenon of today's Black-Eyed Children mirrors Wyndham's sinister story of yesteryear.

Don't Let Them In

Who, or what, the Black-Eyed Children (BEC) are, is a matter that has had the paranormal and UFO research communities occupied for several years. Before we get to the nature and potential intent of the BEC, let's first take a look at their appearance—which is, without doubt, eerie in the extreme. Typically, the BEC appear to range in age from around 10 to 14. They are, more often than not, male. They are acutely skinny and pale in the extreme. Their preferred color of clothing is black, and almost always a black hoodie that envelops—and hides—most of their face. Then there is the matter of why they are named the Black-Eyed Children. Put simply, their eyes are black. And we're not just talking about portions of the eye. No. The *entire eye* is black. Their intent is curiously identical in practically every case on record: They try and find any way possible to enter the home or the vehicle of the person they target. Because most of the people who have encountered the BEC are terrified out of their wits by the appearances of their strange visitors, they seldom, if ever, allow them entry—which means we are pretty much at a loss to understand *why* it's so important for the BEC to gain access to peoples' property.

As for the theories for what the Black-Eyed Children might be, they range from predatory vampires to energy-sucking ghosts, and from demonic beings to fairy-like changelings. Then there is the theory that they are just the latest, unearthly addition to the alien bloodline. It's important to note that, unlike some of the hybrid children that alien abductees report encountering (discussed in the previous chapter), there is simply no way that the BEC can pass among us unnoticed. The hybrid children may look somewhat strange and sickly, but they are not always overly alien-looking. The blank, black eyes of the BEC, however, effectively ensure that no one is going to come away from an encounter with them and think "sickly child." On top of that, the Black-Eyed Children possess the disturbing ability to near-hypnotize people, as they attempt to enforce their malevolent will on their unfortunate victims. With that said, let's take a look at a few standout reports.

Replacing a human baby with a genetically created lookalike.

The Origins of the BEC

Today, there are literally dozens of cases on file concerning the Black-Eyed Children; however, the most important one of all, is, of course, the first case—or, at least, the first *reported* case. It comes from a man named Brian Bethel, a respected journalist, whose story first began to circulate in 1998. As fate would have it, on the night in question, Bethel, of Abilene, Texas, realized he had forgotten to pay a bill, so he got in his vehicle with the intent of depositing a check in an after-hours drop-box. It was coming up to 10 p.m. when Bethel arrived at the location, which was situated at a shopping mall. As Bethel sat in his vehicle writing out the check, he was interrupted in terrifying style by a loud tapping on the driver's window.

As he quickly looked up, Bethel was confronted by a pair of young boys who, at first glance, in the darkness and the shadows, appeared normal. Matters very quickly became deeply strange, however. In no time at all, Bethel developed a disturbing sense that all was not well. It was as if a malignant atmosphere had suddenly descended and blanketed his vehicle, and as if out of nowhere. Bethel was careful to only wind the window down to a small degree, and asked the boys what they wanted. They came up with a story that sounded most unlikely and left Bethel feeling very uneasy—frightened, even. They claimed to need a ride back home, so that they could get some money and then go to see a movie.

"C'mon, mister. Let us in. We can't get in your car until you do, you know," said one. It was at this point that Bethel finally saw the eyes of the pair. They were completely black, with no iris or pupil anywhere in sight. Bethel knew exactly what he had to do: He hit the accelerator and was gone. And so were the BEC. As Bethel looked back, they had seemingly vanished, and impossibly quickly, too (Weatherly, 2012).

Black Eyes at the Door

Experiences like that of Brian Bethel abound. In 2011, I investigated the case of a woman named Alison who had a very similar experience in the previous year (2010) at an Orange County, California, strip motel. It was around 11 p.m. when a loud knock at the door made Alison practically jump out of her skin—as, at the time, she was laid out on the bed, engrossed in a movie. Rather weirdly, the movie was Roman Polanski's 1967 movie, *Rosemary's Baby*, which tells the story of a woman who gives birth to a demonic baby. Alison tentatively got up and tiptoed to the door, peering through the spyhole. She could see two young boys, both in black hoodies, stood right in front of the door.

As if realizing that Alison was silently, and worriedly, watching them, one of the boys leaned into the spyhole and said, "Please let us in. We need to use the telephone." Not only did the request send shivers throughout Alison's body, but the fact that the boy deliberately kept his face pointed downward, while looming into view, and his eyes in shadow only added to the menace (Redfern, 2014).

Then, something very disturbing happened: Alison felt as if an evil force was taking over her own self-will and was trying to make her open the door to her late-night callers of the sinister kind. It took a supreme effort on Alison's part not to unlock and open the door. Fortunately, she was able to fight off what became, she said, a "need" to let the children in. Having regained her wits and sense of self-preservation, Alison looked again through the spyhole, only to see the boy staring right at her *through a pair of solid black eyes*. She screamed, jumped back, and called the night manager, who was on the scene in no time at all. The BEC were nowhere in sight (Ibid.).

Men in Black and Vampires: The BEC Parallels

It's worth noting another UFO connection in the uncanny saga of the Black-Eyed Children: They have deep parallels to the notorious Men in Black, who have, since 1947, terrorized and intimidated into silence numerous witnesses to UFOs. Just like the BEC, the Men in Black have a propensity for knocking on doors late at night. The two mirror each other in other fashions, too. Like their child counterparts, the MIB will not enter a home until they are specifically invited to do so (shades of ancient vampire lore). Both the MIB and the BEC wear black. Both wear head-gear: hoodies for the Black-Eyed Children, and 1950s-era fedoras for the MIB. And there is another intriguing issue: Very often the Men in Black wear thick, wraparound, black sunglasses. One has to wonder if this is done not just to provoke a menacing atmosphere, but to mask a pair of emotion-free, solid, black eyes. In that sense, and just perhaps, the Men in Black and the Black-Eyed Children are one and the same: one in adult form and the other in child form, but both following the same secret agenda—whatever that may really be. So, where does that all leave us? Well, it admittedly leaves us with a lot of questions. But they are questions that a certain acclaimed and dedicated researcher of the Black-Eyed Children has done his very best to resolve.

Undoubtedly the leading investigator in this field, and the author of the book *The Black Eyed Children*, David Weatherly has collected and studied dozens of such cases, demonstrating the sheer scale of these weird and unsettling events. Weatherly's work has addressed a variety of theories for the presence of the BEC: that they might be demonic in nature, or predatory spirits, or possibly even products of the human mind, given some semblance of physical life in the real world. Notably, Weatherly has also spent much time researching the theory that the Black-Eyed Children are of nothing less than an alien bloodline. Weatherly cites the case of two women, Ann and Marcia, who have both had alien abduction experiences and who have also both encountered the BEC—and, in Marcia's case, in the now-typical "knocking on the door and demanding to be let in" situation.

Of cases such as these, Weatherly says: "Why would an alien race want, or need, to create hybrid beings? There are a number of proposed theories to explain why such an experiment may be taking place. These theories range from a dying race that needs an injection of fresh DNA in order to survive, to time travelers attempting to correct a mistake made in their past (which is our present) (Weatherly, 2012).

We will leave the final words on this issue to Weatherly. They are words that fit comfortably with what we have seen so far: "An even more sinister theory that has followers, postulates that the grays are actually attempting to take over our world by slowly breeding us out and phasing in beings with alien DNA. Over time the human race will fade away to be replaced by the 'superior' DNA of the gray aliens, adherents say" (Ibid.).

Reptiles From the Stars

It was in the 1980s that a new, mysterious and, for some, down-right sinister development occurred within the field of UFO research. More and more people, predominantly women, began to report alien abduction encounters of a kind very different to those involving the Grays. In these newly surfaced cases, the experiencers reported abductions at the hands and claws of what one might con-sider to be the closest, real-life equivalents of the scaly beast in the 1954 movie *Creature From the Black Lagoon*. Some called them Lizard Men; others referred to them as being dinosaur-like in appearance. But the one term that really struck a chord—to the extent that it was soon adopted by both UFO researchers and conspiracy theorists alike—was Reptilians.

There is a near-unanimous belief that there is absolutely nothing positive, at all, about the Reptilians. Alien abduction researcher John Carpenter says of this ominous breed of beast:

Typically, these reptilian creatures are reported to be about six to seven feet tall, upright, with lizard-like scales, green-ish to brownish in color with claw-like, four-fingered webbed hands. Their faces are said to be a cross between a human and a snake, with a central ridge coming down from the top of the head to the snout. Adding to their serpent-like appearance are their eyes which have vertical slits in their pupils and golden irises (Carpenter, 1993).

Lizard Men and Genetics

The Reptilians are shape-shifting, extraterrestrial monsters that have lived among us since time immemorial. As a result of their abilities to take on human form, they have completely infiltrated society, governments, and military and intelligence agencies. None other than the British royal family, and countless famous figures of Hollywood and the music industry are terrible Reptilians masquerading as humans! They are the true, secret rulers of our world, machinating and manipulating as they coldly see fit. They are also the human-like Anunnaki, albeit in a different form, due to their ability to shape-shift, not unlike the classic werewolf of medieval lore. Or, so we are assured by some of the most extreme, conspiracy-minded.

Trying to determine where the truth behind the Reptilian agenda begins, and the wild and completely unsubstantiated and unsupported claims take over, is no easy task. But of one thing we can be certain: There is a huge body of data and testimony that makes it clear the Reptilians have a connection to the alien abduction phenomenon of today and to the Anunnaki of the distant past—which means, despite the inflammatory nature of the Reptilian controversy, we have no choice but to address it.

The Anunnaki and the Reptilians

Before we get to the matter of the Reptilians in the modern era, and their undeniable connections to alien abductions, shape-shifting, inter-species sex, reproduction, and hybrid entities, it's important that we address something of extreme relevance and importance: the connection between the Reptilians and none other than the Anunnaki, and the astounding possibility that they just might be one and the same. It's a connection that takes us back in time several thousand years and to the world of the Mesoamericans—the people of Honduras, El Salvador, Belize, Costa Rica, Mexico, and Guatemala—and a powerful and mysterious character known as Quetzalcoatl, who may well have been of Anunnaki lineage.

According to predominantly Aztec legend, Quetzalcoatl was a highly advanced entity, with near-magical skills and possessed of incredibly advanced sciences, who tried to bring civilization, technology, and a new world to the Mesoamericans, and who first impacted on the people of the area at some point between 100 BC and 100 AD. His name translates as "feathered serpent"—hence the name of a notable structure that can be found at Teotihuacan, just a short drive from Mexico City, and that was built around 100 BC: the Temple of the Feathered Serpent.

Admittedly, there is some degree of controversy over the precise date upon which Quetzalcoatl first surfaced—and for one, specific reason: Long before Quetzalcoatl was on the scene, and as far back as 900 BC, Mesoamericans were worshipping *other* serpentine deities, and particularly so in Tabasco, Mexico. It is this matter of a serpentine deity-like entity that has led investigators of the Reptilian phenomenon to make a connection between Quetzalcoatl of times long past and the Reptilians of today's UFO lore.

In both written texts and ancient artwork, Quetzalcoatl is portrayed—particularly so by the Aztecs—as both a very human-looking entity (dark hued and displaying a reddish beak, which is a nod in the direction of the god of wind, Ehacatl) and as a serpentine, feathered, creature that displays bright and eye-catching plumage—hence the meaning of his name. This decidedly curious state of extreme duality has prompted a theory that suggests Quetzalcoatl was a shape-shifter of the reptilian kind, one who was identical to, and directly related to, the body-morphing Reptilians of today's alien-abduction controversy.

Aliens of the Reptilian Kind.

The Quetzalcoatl Connection Continues

Whereas the legends of the Anunnaki suggest their presence on the Earth dates back hundreds of thousands of years, Quetzalcoatl, as noted by the time frame in which he first surfaced in Mesoamerica, was very much an Anunnaki of the Johnny-come-lately type. Or was he?

Zechariah Sitchin concluded, from studying and comparing ancient Mesoamerican texts with those of the Sumerians, that Quetzalcoatl was none other than the offspring of Enki, who was one of the original, central players in the genetic manipulation of the infant human race by the Anunnaki. That the Anunnaki reputedly had the ability to live for hundreds of thousands of years means it's not at all impossible that, as Enki's son, Quetzalcoatl—who felt that the human race should be treated fairly and not used as a slave-based society—lived throughout the *entirety* of incredible and turbulent times: the decision to travel to the Earth and reap its gold; the creation of a new human species; the mighty flood that decimated the Earth; and the return of the vast majority of the Anunnaki to their home planet of Nibiru.

Researchers such as Zechariah Sitchin have suggested that the Anunnaki left the Earth more than 4,000 years ago, which is long before Quetzalcoatl was on the scene in Mesoamerica. Or did the Anunnaki—or, at least, some of them—choose to stay on the Earth after the decimation provoked by massive, worldwide floods and localized atomic conflict? Certainly, that is what Sitchin suggested: *Some of the Anunnaki remained behind.* Perhaps, even, the smaller, remaining colony provoked a radical change in their relationship to, and interaction with, the human race. It may well have been to the extent that the once-all-powerful Anunnaki—perceived and worshipped for so very long as gods—took a backseat, retreated into the shadows, and adopted a far more covert and stealthy approach to future genetic alteration and upgrading of the human species. Certainly, that would accord *exactly* with today's world of alien abductions: Just about each and every aspect of just about each and every abduction is performed in stealthy fashion and with a desire— not always successful, as we have seen—to wipe out the memories of those unfortunate souls they target.

If a sizeable number of Anunnaki did remain on the Earth, just perhaps, one of them was Quetzalcoatl. And maybe he elected to try to help the survivors of the planetary disaster rebuild and reinvent themselves, via the introduction of new technologies and concepts— specifically in Mesoamerica. He may have played some sort of role in the genetic programs, too. On this matter of genetics, Paul Von

Ward, the author of *We've Never Been Alone*, noted that the Quinault people of the Pacific Northwest believed their god, Kwatee, "created humans from his own sweat," and that in the American west, the Selish people have a story that their creator-entity, Amotken, used his very own hair to create the first five women on Earth. "All these methods," said Von Ward, "could imply a contribution of the gods' DNA." And all of which brings us to Von Ward's words on Quetzalcoatl: according to legend, Quetzalcoatl "sprinkled his blood with the bones of earlier creatures to create humans" (Von Ward, 2011).

"Reptilians Are Not a Politically Correct Species"

Without doubt, the most vocal person, when it comes to the matter of human-Reptilian interaction, is Pamela Stonebrooke. A jazz-singer known as the "Intergalactic Diva" and whose music CD, *Experiencer*, was based on her numerous encounters with the green, scaly creatures, Stonebrooke has an almost-unique take on the Reptilian phenomenon. Robert Sterling, of the now-defunct magazine *The Excluded Middle*, said: "Stonebrooke isn't particularly unique for having claimed to have sex with lizard aliens. What makes her story special is that she seems to have really enjoyed it" (Sterling, 1999).

Indeed, it was this aspect of Stonebrooke's encounters of the deeply intense and personal type that provoked a wave of criticism from some of the more closed-minded, uptight, and unenlightened souls in UFO research. It was criticism that led Stonebrooke, to her credit, not to slink away into the shadows, but to firmly stand up against her detractors and send out an open-letter to the entire field of Ufology. In part, it stated:

> Reptilians are not a politically correct species in the UFO community, and to admit to having sex with one—much less enjoying it—is beyond the pale as far as the more conservative members of that community are concerned. But I know

from my extensive reading and research, and from talking personally to dozens of other women (and men) that I am not unique in reporting this kind of experience...

I am the first to admit that this is a vastly complex subject, a kind of hall of mirrors, where dimensional realities are constantly shifting and changing. Certainly, the reptilians use sex to control people in various ways. They have the ability to shape-shift and to control the mind of the experiencer, as well as to give tremendous pleasure through their mental powers. I have wrestled with all of these implications and the various levels of meaning and possibilities represented by my encounter experiences. I will say, however, as I have said before, that I feel a deep respect for the reptilian entity with whom I interacted, and a profound connection with this being (Ibid.).

Stonebrooke also had something to say that might well have had a bearing on some of the legends pertaining to the Anunnaki and their downfall on planet Earth, when Nibiru made its catastrophic passing, close to the Earth: "In a past life regression I did recently, I went to a very remote period in earth's history (perhaps hundreds of thousands of years ago), and saw myself as one of a brotherhood of reptilian warriors facing a catastrophic event in which we perished together (it was possibly nuclear in nature, since I saw a red cloud and felt tremendous heat)" (Ibid.).

Master and Servant

As Stonebrooke noted in her open letter, she was hardly what one could term a solitary soul in the matter of the Reptilians and the sexual component of alien abduction accounts. She was correct: Such cases abound. Liz is a 38-year-old school-teacher living in Anaheim, California. Since the age of 19, Liz has had experiences that can only be described as ranging from the fear-inducing to the mind-blowing.

Like so many abductees—and whether at the hands of the Grays or the Reptilians—on the no-less-than 17 occasions upon which Liz was taken from her home, she has only the very haziest of memories of how she was taken on-board what she was absolutely sure was an alien spacecraft. Also on every occasion, those engaged in the abduction were the Grays. It quickly became clear to Liz, however, that the Grays were little more than the equivalent of worker bees, dutifully and unquestioningly following the orders of their overlords, the Reptilians. This much was obvious to Liz: Whenever she found herself coming out of a state that she described as being similar to anesthesia, she would see at least two creatures—"like large lizards," said Liz—apparently overseeing the procedures that the Grays were performing in almost robotic, programmed fashion. Those procedures, solely of a gynecological nature, were always fear-filled, painful, distressing, and nightmare-inducing for weeks later (Redfern, 2013).

On 11 out of the 17 occasions, says Liz, she awoke, on a large table, to find herself being penetrated by a huge, male, reptilian humanoid. She is of the opinion that the creature held some form of significant sway over her mind, because she did not find the experience at all terrifying—as one might expect most people to find, if pinned down and forced to have sex with something akin to a goliath-sized, bipedal alligator. Like Pamela Stonebrooke, Liz experienced powerful orgasms and thoroughly enjoyed the acts, which, in her own words, she described as being of a "master and servant" nature. And to the extent that not unlike a junkie in need of the next, better fix, Liz found herself craving reptilian sex—again and again (Ibid.).

Whereas Liz feels, today, that the gynecological procedures were specifically undertaken to secure DNA and eggs from her body, and were part of a larger, overall, important agenda focused on human-alien reproduction, she was equally certain that the Reptilians had sex with her for one very simply reason and one alone: They wanted to because they enjoy it. And one final thing: Liz's blood-type is O Negative.

Terror in the Land of Enchantment

At the other end of the scale is the case of Annika, a now-married woman from Taos, New Mexico, whose sexual liaisons with the Reptilians were filled with stone-cold terror. Now 43, Annika had just two encounters of the green and scaly kind, both near the New Mexican town of Dulce, which has a long history of UFO sightings, cattle mutilations, and even claims of a vast, alien installation buried deep inside Archuleta Mesa, which dominates the Dulce landscape.

In 2001, and in her late 20s and single at the time, Annika was seeing a man who lived in Dulce, approximately a 120-mile drive from Taos on US-64W. On both occasions when the abductions occurred, the time was late at night and the location was the same: while she was driving through the Carson National Forest, through which US-64W cuts a swathe.

On both occasions, Annika experienced the typical alien abduction scenario that began with first seeing a strange light, hanging low in the sky. That was followed by a close-up encounter with a large, saucer-shaped object, and then a sense of feeling drugged, the car coming to a grinding halt, and her transfer to what she assumed was the interior of the same object, where she found herself tied to a cold, metallic table—where she, like Liz, was subjected to a gynecological procedure that was both painful and fear-inducing.

Also on both occasions, that fear was elevated to absolutely stratospheric proportions when the trio of Grays exited the room and a large—8- to 9-feet-tall—Reptilian entered the picture. Somewhat notably, Annika says that the entity—she was sure it was the same one each time—was dressed in a robe that displayed multiple, small images of what she termed "a snake with wings." This, recall, is a very close description of Quetzalcoatl, the winged serpent and the alleged son of Enku of the Anunnaki—and also of the emblem that Herbert Schirmer's talkative alien displayed on his uniform on a fateful, dark night in Ashland, Nebraska, in December 1967 (Redfern, interview, 2015).

Each night was the same: The creature casually disrobed and walked over to the table, which was tilted to a semi-upright position, and Annika felt her legs pushed apart and her knees pushed up. The lizard-like thing penetrated Annika in violent fashion, causing nothing but pain and terror, something that continued for seven or eight minutes at most, after which the creature ejaculated and in seconds exited the room. Annika's next memories were of sitting in the driver's seat of her car, her clothes in disarray, and a burning sensation in her vagina. It was only when she saw a television documentary on the Reptilian phenomena that Annika realized that the experience she remembered was acutely similar to numerous additional people, all across the United States.

Military Abductions and Rh Negative Blood

If a significant percentage of the world's population—the Rh negatives—is not entirely human, logic dictates that it would surely be a matter of some deep concern to worldwide governments, military bodies, and intelligence agencies. Regardless of the extent (large or small) to which agencies might view the Rh negative controversy as a valid one, at the very least we should see some degree of careful monitoring of the situation by those in positions of power and influence. And, guess what? *We do*. Welcome to the world of the "MILABS," a term that, in effect, means "military abductions."

If you thought it was the extraterrestrials abducting sizeable numbers of the world's population, for possibly deeply disturbing reasons of a genetics-based nature, you would be right. There is, however, another category of abductors: those attached to a covert arm of the U.S. military that, in essence, abducts the abductees— many of the Rh negative bloodline—to see what can be learned from their experiences about the alien agenda. That same covert arm may also be deeply worried about the rise of the Black-Eyed Children and the hybrids.

Spying on the Abductees

For decades, abductees have reported what appears to be hard evidence of clandestine surveillance by military personnel. Black and unmarked helicopters are often seen flying over the homes of abductees. Mail is intercepted, opened, and then resealed—in a fashion that is clearly done for effect, for purposes of intimidation and, in a far from subtle situation, letting the abductees know they are being watched. Telephone interference, including strange noises and voices on the line, are widespread. Black cars, with tinted windows, follow people around town. That's nothing compared to being abducted, however. To be taken against one's will by emotionless, drone-like aliens is one thing; to then have the distinct misfortune of being abducted by military personnel as a result, *too*, is just adding to the insult.

Secret military surveillance of the Rh negatives.

The world of alien-abduction research is absolutely filled with such cases, to the extent that this is clearly not just the result of the claims of a few, overly paranoid figures peering through the curtains and interpreting every passing vehicle as belonging to "the government."

Most intriguing of all, it becomes clear from a careful study of the words and recollections of the MILAB victims that their military, human abductors know a great deal about the Rh negative phenomenon. We have already seen how, as far back as the 1950s, the CIA was recommending that African gold mines should be monitored for any evidence of UFO activity in the immediate vicinity. Someone, it would appear, knew at least *something* of the gold/mining/UFO links more than half a century ago; how exactly, is a matter of mystery. It may well be the case, however, this this knowledge—hazy or substantial—prompted the establishment of the MILAB programs, as a means to try and further officialdom's knowledge of the Anunnaki and the Rh negatives.

As will soon become clear, the suspicion that there are those in positions of power who know something of the Earth's forgotten and misinterpreted history, is most apparent by the questions that those attached to the MILAB programs ask the people they interrogate. They very often relate to matters concerning blood, genetics, DNA, and hybrid entities. It's both interesting and disturbing to note, too, that the MILAB interrogators regularly ask the abductees if they have any knowledge of long-term, possibly hostile agendas on the part of the aliens, and specifically in relation to the hybrid beings. This issue, of future events, of what we might call ET-controlled "sleeper agents," and of the Rh negative link to these matters is something that cannot be ignored.

It's time, now, for us to take a look at what is, beyond any shadow of doubt, evidence of widespread surveillance of the abductees. Then, we will spread our wings further, as we force open the doors behind which are hidden the U.S. government's most highly classified secrets of the ancient past.

Secret Interest in the Ancient Past

Before we get to the specific matters of the MILABS, and why they are undertaken, it's important to stress that there is a deep precedent to the idea of government agencies secretly monitoring matters relative to pre-history, archaeology, and religious stories, legends, and fables. My 2012 book, *The Pyramids and the Pentagon*, demonstrated—thanks to the provisions of the Freedom of Information Act—that since 1947, the CIA has taken a close interest in the Dead Sea Scrolls. In 1949, the CIA and the U.S. Air Force opened files on the controversy surrounding the alleged landing spot of Noah's Ark on Mount Ararat, Turkey. In the early 1960s, the CIA created a dossier on the matter of the Ark of the Covenant. The U.S. Navy and the Army both have file collections that address the question of whether or not the Pyramids of Giza, Egypt, were constructed by the use of a poorly understood form of levitation or anti-gravity.

What this tells us is that someone in officialdom knows something of the connection between ancient aliens and our civilization's most enduring, biblical accounts, artifacts, and mysteries. And they have known since at least 1947. Keeping that in mind—particularly so the fact that the tale of Noah's Ark is a direct part of the story of the Anunnaki—it makes perfect sense for some clandestine agency of the government—or more likely, of the military—to turn its attentions to the matter of the Rh negatives and their ancient, controversial origins.

Kidnapped and Interrogated

As far as can be determined, MILAB-based activity dates back to at least 1980. One of the most significant, and graphic, cases involved a woman named Myrna Hansen, who had a notable and controversial UFO encounter late one night while driving to New Mexico, after vacationing in Oklahoma. After realizing that a substantial amount of time seemed to be missing from the journey, and having vague, UFO-related memories concerning the night's events, she underwent hypnosis to try to determine what had taken place. It transpires that she was abducted by a group of small, black-eyed aliens that took her on board a UFO, on which she was treated in a fashion very similar to that of Betty and Barney Hill back in 1961.

That is to say, as the human equivalent of a lab rat. In many respects, what happened next was even weirder.

Hansen's hypnotically retrieved memories revealed that, when the aliens were done with her, she was taken to some form of subterranean installation. This was no alien base, however. What it actually was, was something quite different. When word of Hansen's experience and recollections began to circulate among Ufologists, sources at Kirtland Air Force Base, New Mexico, who were secretly following the story, instantly realized that what Hansen had described was—rather incredibly—a classified, off-limits bunker that was a part of the base's weapons storage area.

The implication—given that Hansen was not an employee of the Air Force, and as a result, did not have a security clearance to access the weapons storage area—was that elements of the military were monitoring the alien abduction, and then, when it was over, flew Hansen, in a darkened helicopter, to Kirtland, where she was subjected to a grilling by military personnel, demanding to know what occurred while she was on the UFO. Whatever the Air Force learned, it remains unknown outside of the world of the underground domain of the MILABS.

The Black Helicopter Component

In an earlier chapter, the case of Betty Andreasson was addressed. A woman with a lifetime of anomalous, alien abduction–themed incidents, she was—as will be recalled—the recipient in the 1960s of messages from extraterrestrials that spoke, rather curiously, in a form of the Gaelic language. The Gaels and the Celts, as we have seen, have an ancestral lineage that is traceable to the Basque people of France and Spain, who, in turn, are the closest living equivalents of the Cro-Magnons—who were the genetically mutated puppets of the Anunnaki. Remember, too, that Andreasson is of Finnish-English origin, and the people of Finland are known for their above average numbers of Rh negatives, and particularly those of the Type O variety.

All of this makes the next revelation all the more intriguing: Betty Andreasson has not only had a lifetime of UFO encounters; she has had repeated run-ins with the notorious black helicopter phenomenon. Betty's husband, Bob, has been able to take quite literally hundreds of photos of these particular craft in the direct vicinity of the Andreasson home. The clear and repeated harassment provoked Bob to fire off a blistering letter to the Army, demanding to know what the hell was going on. The response was an astounding one: The military kept things short and to the point, stating that it was "difficult" for them to say anything, because even the Army was unable to figure out who was flying the helicopters. "Go away," in other words (Fawcett and Greenwood, 1984).

A Doctor Gets Placed Under Surveillance

The late Dr. Karla Turner was the author of a number of books about her very own, and deeply personal, alien abduction experiences, including *Into the Fringe* and *Taken: Inside the Alien-Human Abduction Agenda*. In the early to mid-1990s, respected UFO researcher and authority Greg Bishop had extensive mail correspondence with Dr. Turner on the alien abduction controversy. Of note, every single piece of correspondence between the pair arrived torn open and resealed. Someone was taking note.

It's almost certainly no coincidence that Turner's husband, Casey, reported a MILAB abduction. Although the precise date and location to which he was taken remain unknown, Casey described being taken to a below-ground facility, where he witnessed several other people, like him, drugged and the subject of interrogation. He offered the opinion: "I get the feeling they want to know, maybe they're trying to find out what it is we know" (Turner, 1992).

An Rh negative Abductee Speaks

Researcher Katharina Wilson has dug deep into the connections between alien abductees, MILABS, and the Rh negative phenomenon. One of her sources was a woman named Lisa, who revealed something of extraordinary value to this issue—possibly something that was of interest to those in the military monitoring the Rh negative situation. Wilson said to Lisa: "You state in your journal that despite being raised a Christian, someone—possibly the beings themselves—have told you that you are really Jewish. I read this several times in your journal. I find this very interesting and I was wondering if you could elaborate on this? Does this occur during MILAB encounters, alien encounters or both?" (Wilson, 2008).

Lisa replied:

I am a Christian and also a Jew. I feel so saddened because I sense I am hated for being both. They told me I am a Hidden Jew. I didn't know what that meant until I looked it up. It means, "Thru the Blood you will be known [me and others]. That is how they will hunt you down."…

Then, when I'm with the military [MILAB experience] they call me a Jewish Wench. Years ago during an encounter I was told they would try and find every last one of us through our DNA and that our blood tells so much about who we are. My blood type is B negative, and I believe the RH-negative blood is of importance no matter what part of the human race you are (Ibid.).

Communion Attracts Secret Attention

Moving on, we have the very curious saga of journalist Ed Conroy. He is the author of *Report on Communion*, published in 1989, a study of Conroy's own personal investigation of the events detailed in Whitley Strieber's 1987 best-seller, *Communion*. Conroy took a welcome, unbiased, and detached approach to the subject—that is, until he found that he unwittingly became a player in the saga himself. Like Betty Andreasson and so many others, Conroy was targeted by the people behind the black helicopter conundrum. As just one example of many, Conroy said that in 1988 he noticed "an uncanny apparent connection between my telephone conversations and the appearance of the helicopters. On more than one occasion when I had entered into a conversation regarding the subject of UFOs and/ or the visitors, a helicopter flew into view." More amazingly, and on the topic of his *Report on Communion*, Conroy recalled: "A small Bell 47-type helicopter also appeared out my window immediately after the telephone conversation with my agent in which I accepted the terms for the contract for this book" (Conroy, 1989).

MILABS and Monsters

The following case is a fascinating one, as it echoes Zechariah Sitchin's thoughts on the possibility that ancient accounts of Centaurs, Cyclops, and Minotaur may have been prompted by bizarre experiments involving the hybridization of various species. Therapist Barbara Bartholic regressed an alien abduction victim named Fred, who later had MILABS experiences and who told her of a bizarre encounter involving an unknown animal: "I feel like they are doing something to me with the animal. They are doing something with my blood, my sperm and my genes. They are injecting fluids into this animal. Then I remember seeing another type of animal running around. I can't remember what the animal looked like, but it was bizarre. Seems like the animal is part human and part animal" (Lammer and Lammer, 1999).

A Reptilian Component

We even have the controversial matter of the so-called Reptilians surfacing in the MILABS mystery. MILABS expert Dr. Helmut Lammer and his wife, Marion, have closely followed this issue and have secured literally hundreds of cases of military abduction. One concerns a woman named Michelle, whose MILABS experience—at the hands of what appeared to be military person-nel, and who took her into a darkened room that resembled an office—involved a traumatic, fear-filled encounter with something terrifying: a Reptilian. Interviewed by a Dr. Kougell, PhD, a hyp-notherapist who was able to reach into Michelle's mind and extract the salient, sensational facts, Michelle described seeing in the room: "...a creature about 6–7 feet tall. His ears are large and pointed at the top. His eyes are bright yellow-gold and seem to glow. He has pointy teeth and a large wrinkle on his forehead and he has a tail" (Ibid.).

Fringe cases like this one only serve to confuse and inflame the subject of MILABS ever further. Yet, as we have seen, both the Reptilians and tailed-beings—including babies born with tail-like appendages—are both aspects of the overall story of the Rh negatives.

"They Took an Awful Lot of Blood"

Then there is the 1987 experience of Brenda. A resident of Houston, Texas, she has conscious recall of encounters, in the family home, with dwarfish, gray-skinned extraterrestrials dating back to early childhood—encounters that exposed her to graphic end-of-the-world-style imagery. Brenda also has fragmentary memories of alien abduction events, which began in her early teens and extended until right around the time when menopause began, in the late 1990s.

As for the 1987 encounter, Brenda—who is Rh negative, Type O—was driving late at night to visit family in the southeast Texan city of Beaumont. She arrived fine, but not until the following morning. Her family was frantic and was all but ready to contact the police when it became clear that something—something deeply worrying—was going on. It was only Brenda's call from a 24-hour gas station, in the early hours of the morning, that prevented the authorities from being brought in and a full-scale manhunt being initiated.

When Brenda finally reached her family, it was clear she was in a state of deep distress and utter confusion. Concerned that she had been attacked, mugged, or worse, her brother wanted to bring the police in—immediately. Brenda pleaded otherwise and explained what she consciously recalled. It was not much, but it revolved around being taken from her car—by what seemed to be military personnel—who she believed had somehow been able to "prompt" her into exiting the main highway from Houston to Beaumont and down a lonely stretch of heavily wooded road, where she was confronted by a black van, surrounded by a group of four or five men, all dressed in black fatigues. Brenda also recalled being taken, in what she felt was a drugged state, to a small, sub-surface facility, a couple of miles away at the very most, where she was interrogated in downright-hostile fashion by two elderly men whom she perceived as being doctors. They were doctors surrounded by several men in military uniforms that befitted the likes of generals.

The two doctors, Brenda says, "...wanted to know, did I know my blood group? Well, yes I did. They took a lot of blood. Vials. They kept asking me about my blood: Did I get a lot of nosebleeds? Did I have any physical differences? I don't know what that meant. Did I feel like I was on a mission to do things for the aliens? Well, I have *always* thought that and I told them. I remember the doctors looking at each other when I said that" (Redfern, interview with Brenda, 2014).

Brenda is sure that there was more to the encounter, and to the question-and-answer session, too, than she can consciously recall. She is not, however, willing to undergo hypnosis, fearful of the possibility that doing so will bring out more of the facts and plunge her into greater depths of anxiety than she found herself on that strange and traumatic night in southeast Texas.

One final thing, for reasons that she remains admittedly unsure, Brenda sensed that the underground facility was what she termed "temporary." She qualified this with the following: "I got the feeling this place, whatever it might have been, was abandoned—for a long time. It was convenient, I guess, for them to use somewhere and not get caught" (Ibid.).

This is a fascinating, albeit brief, revelation. It suggests that whoever is running the MILABS program does so outside of specific government and congressional oversight. Or, it may be that private corporations are hired, covertly, to undertake the interrogations, thereby preventing any kind of paper trail from leading back to some element of the military or government that may be financing it. Using abandoned facilities, and ensuring that no same place is utilized twice when it comes to the interrogation of the Rh negatives, may explain why it has proved to be so difficult to find and track the movements of the MILABS teams. They are constantly on the move, funded by covert and black-budget-based projects, answerable to no one, and, for all intents and purposes, non-existing. No doubt, that's just how they like it. It's of no liking to the Rh negatives, however, who constantly find themselves at the mercy of intrusive MILABS teams.

Rh Negatives: Us Vs. Them

One of the most fascinating—but also disturbing—aspects of the Rh negative phenomenon is that those with this particular blood group display certain physical characteristics that, though they are certainly not unique to these particular people alone, are most certainly more prevalent than in the rest of the population. We'll start with the more down-to-earth aspects, and then work our way on up to the undeniably astonishing ones.

In terms of brainpower and intelligence, Rh negative individuals have been shown to have significantly greater than average IQ levels. It's not at all unlikely (in fact, it's highly *likely*) that this stems from their connection to the Cro-Magnons, and the fact that Cro-Magnon man had a brain approximately 10-percent greater in size than any other human that has ever existed—and that includes *Homo sapiens*. To put that into its correct and understandable context, Cro-Magnon man's brain exceeded the size of a modern-day human brain by somewhere in the region of a tennis ball, as incredible as that might sound.

From the days when the earliest humans walked the earth, and including the time frame in which Cro-Magnons dominated much of Western Europe, the human brain grew progressively larger. It may surprise many to learn that this is not the case now. University of Wisconsin anthropologist John Hawks has commented on this issue. He says of how the human brain expanded in size as the millennia passed by: "That was true for two million of our evolution. But there has been a reversal. And it's also clear the brain has been shrinking" (McAuliffe, 2011).

Indeed, in the last 20,000 years or thereabout, the average human brain has shrunk in size from 1,500 cubic centimeters to 1,350 cc. Whether or not this is an indication of the overall dumbing down of society, and humankind in general, is a matter of debate. Within the field of anthropology there is no solid consensus as to why our brains are shrinking. What we *can* say for sure is that even if human brain mass is on a decline (irreversibly or not), the Rh negatives, at least, appear to have retained their Cro-Magnon-style brainpower.

Rh negatives: Not Fans of the Sun

Then there is the matter of the Rh negatives' inability to tolerate strong sunlight and high temperatures. Specifically, Rh negatives report problems that fall under the category of what is termed *photosensitivity*. In simple terms, it's a condition prompted by sunlight that affects the human immune system. The results can range from the mild to the alarming: Nausea, vertigo, lightheadedness, elevated heart rates, and dizziness are typical. Those affected by photosensitivity can also develop rashes, inflammation, and hives, which may be small and localized to large and widespread, and which can result in mild irritation to intense itchiness.

Somewhat intriguingly, it's almost as if the immunity systems of the Rh negatives are not designed to be exposed to the power and heat of our own Sun. This begs a thought-provoking question: Whose sun, exactly, *were* they designed to operate under? That of ancient, visiting extraterrestrials, perhaps? Given what we know from the time frame of the Cro-Magnons to the present era, such a question is hardly the stretch that some might assume it to be.

Negative Pressure

In today's fast-paced world, one of the major contributing factors to ill health and premature death is high blood pressure. Strokes and heart attacks are often the results of this potentially deadly condition. Present figures demonstrate that approximately seven out of 10 people who have a first heart attack have pre-existing high blood pressure. For first-time stroke victims, it's around eight out of 10. To give an indication of the serious nature of this silent killer—which is proven to be exacerbated by a poor diet, a lack of exercise, and stress—close to 70 million Americans are affected by elevated blood pressure that requires medication to reduce it to safe levels, according to the Centers for Disease Control.

Equally as serious, no less than one in three Americans have blood pressure that is higher than normal, which offers a future potential for their levels to creep steadily into the danger zone. Even more serious, millions of people live with high blood pressure unknowingly; they only become aware of it during routine checks at their doctor's office. Less than 50 percent of those with high blood pressure have their condition under control. And the statistics for deaths associated with, and linked to, high blood pressure are grim in the extreme. As an example, in 2009 alone, there were no less than 348,000 deaths in the United States in which high blood pressure played a role. It's one of the modern world's most lethal conditions.

In terms of which races and ethnic groups are most affected by high blood pressure, the highest proportions are in African Americans, followed by Caucasians, and then by Mexican Americans. There is an exception—one might even be inclined to call it an anomaly—to these statistics. You can, to be sure, see where this story is going.

Rh negatives typically have blood pressure of a slightly lower normal figure than the average 120/80. Blood pressure that is too low can cause alarming conditions, such as dizziness and faintness.

When the figures are somewhat, but not dangerously, lower than average, however, the risks of stroke and heart attack are significantly decreased. It is within this latter, safer domain that the majority of the Rh negatives dwell.

Lower-than-normal body temperatures and heart rates—but with no discernible, adverse effects—are typical, too. Bradycardia, or a slow heartbeat, one that is generally below 60 beats per minute, may be a sign of illness. On the other hand, many athletes have slow heartbeats, due to the fact that they are extremely fit. For example, at the height of his career in the 1970s, tennis legend Bjorn Borg had an average heart rate of only 35 beats a minute. In that sense, the Rh negatives are in extremely good company.

The Saga of the Extra Rib

Now let's take a look at a variety of other, physical issues that make the Rh negatives somewhat different from the rest of the human race. We'll start with the matter of something called thoracic outlet syndrome. It's a medical term that can develop when a person has an extra rib. Most of us have 12 pairs of ribs, which collectively comprise the ribcage. It may come as a surprise to learn that roughly one out of every 200 people are born with an extra rib, known as the cervical rib. Above the first rib and behind the collarbone is the thoracic outlet, which extends from the neck to the armpit. The subclavian artery and vein and the brachial plexus all pass through the thoracic outlet. Thoracic outlet syndrome can occur when that extra rib compresses the thoracic outlet—something that may require surgery to correct. At the very least, physiotherapy and painkillers are needed to lessen the effects of the condition. And among which group of people are more than any other born with that extra rib? The Rh negatives, that's who.

In addition, there is the matter of Adam and Eve. According to the Bible (specifically Genesis 2:18–24) God created the very first woman by removing one of Adam's ribs and then fashioning it into Eve herself. This is in stark contrast to what the Bible tells us about

Adam's origins—namely that he was born specifically out of the dirt of the Earth. Biblical scholars note that God's actions of creating Eve from Adam's rib were prompted by his wish to have people understand that Adam and Eve—man and woman—were two parts of one whole.

It's interesting to note that the ancient Hebrew word for rib was *tsela*. This can, however, also be translated as side, which suggests it was not just Adam's rib that was utilized in the creation of Eve, but also part of the side of his body. This would accord with Adam's words, when he said that Eve was born out of his bones and flesh.

One should not interpret literally the idea that a woman can be magically created from a person's rib. Such a thing is utterly unheard of in medical science. One has to wonder, however, if this particular account is a distortion of some sort of ancient, and highly advanced, surgical procedure that involved the extraction and manipulation of human DNA to create a species that the Bible says began with Adam and Eve, but which might just as easily be interpreted as extraterrestrial manipulation of early Cro-Magnons in Europe, or proto-Cro-Magnons in ancient Africa. Though such a scenario may outrage Christians, let's take a look at what Genesis 2:18–25 actually says:

> Then the Lord God said, "It is not good that the man should be alone; I will make him a helper fit for him." Now out of the ground the Lord God had formed every beast of the field and every bird of the heavens and brought them to the man to see what he would call them. And whatever the man called every living creature, that was its name. The man gave names to all livestock and to the birds of the heavens and to every beast of the field. But for Adam there was not found a helper fit for him. So the Lord God caused a deep sleep to fall upon the man, and while he slept took one of his ribs and closed up its place with flesh. And the rib that the Lord God had taken from the man he made into a woman and brought

her to the man. Then the man said, "This at last is bone of my bones and flesh of my flesh; she shall be called Woman, because she was taken out of Man." Therefore a man shall leave his father and his mother and hold fast to his wife, and they shall become one flesh.

The most significant portion of this biblical extract is the following: "So the Lord God caused a deep sleep to fall upon the man, and while he slept took one of his ribs and closed up its place with flesh" ("Genesis 2:18–25," 2015).

One could very easily—and with significant justification—suggest that the story of God placing Adam into a "deep sleep" was born out of something real, but very different: a primitive human being anaesthetized before surgery, by incredibly advanced extraterrestrials. The analogy is as clear as it is obvious and logical. Whatever the truth of the matter, it's decidedly intriguing that the human rib should play a role in (1) one of the most famous of all the many and varied biblical accounts on human origins, and (2) the physical makeup of so many of the Rh negatives (Ibid.).

Then there is the issue of spinal abnormalities. About one in 10 of the world's population is born with an extra, sixth lumbar vertebra. What is particularly interesting, however, is that the percentage of Rh negatives with an additional vertebra is in excess of 20 percent. Why this should be the case is a mystery, as there are no benefits— or downsides, either—to having one more vertebra than normal. For the Rh negatives, it's simply how things are. It may also account for why the aliens who abducted Barney and Betty Hill spent an inordinate amount of time carefully counting Barney's vertebra.

The Strange Tale of the Tail

Noted expert on conspiracy theories Jim Marrs has observed that "...the tale of human origins linked to extraterrestrials gains even more strength when one considers that many Rh negative children are born with a tail" (Marrs, 2013).

Esther Inglis-Arkell says on the matter of tail-wielding humans:

Some hold with the theory that the development of an embryo shows the stages of evolution. In other words, what first develops is fishlike, and then like a small mammal, and then like a lemur or ape, and then something we would recognize as human. Very early embryos have what look like little gill slits in the beginning of their development. At about four weeks, embryos have a little tail. At around six to twelve weeks, the white blood cells dissolve the tail, and the fetus develops into an average, tail-less baby...most of the time, at least (Inglis-Arkell, 2012).

It is Inglis-Arkell's "most of the time" comment we'll now focus upon. Throughout history there are accounts of babies being born with tails—usually male babies, rather than females, for reasons that remain not completely understood. In some cases, at least, the reason is a wholly down to earth one, such as the "tail" actually being the only visible presence of a parasitic, unborn twin, a tumor (cancerous or benign), or a cyst. When a *true* tail develops, however, it's a throwback to our very earliest ancestors and is caused by the baby's white blood cells failing to absorb, before birth, the relevant tissue of which the tail is comprised (Ibid.).

One example of this aspect of the controversy is that of Balaji, an Indian boy born in 2001 who, at the base of his spine, had nothing less than a 10-centimeter-long tail. People flocked to see Balaji when rumors quickly, and wildly, circulated that he was none other than the reincarnated Hindu monkey-faced god, Lord Hanuman.

It's notable that in some cases the tails are functional; that's to say they contain fat, nerves, and muscle tissue. The result is that they can be controlled and flicked around, in a fashion not unlike that of a dog or a cat. Others hang limply and are completely useless. As for the reason why we see so little evidence of the condition today, it's very simple: We have the medical expertise to remove the tails at birth.

Of relevance to this is the matter of what is called the *cauda equina*. It translates into English as "the tail of a horse." It describes a collection of nerves that extend beyond the spinal column. As for the name, it is derived from the fact that the collection of nerve tracts at the base of the spine looks very much like the tail of a horse. Cauda equina syndrome is a serious and distressing condition that results in the nerves of the spinal cord, contained within the spinal canal, becoming compressed. This can lead to a variety of problems, including numbness, both bladder and bowel incontinence, and sciatica. Surgical decompression is generally the most profitable form of treatment and is vital in the prevention of permanent incontinence.

Jim Marrs notes that some babies of an Rh negative nature "are born with an extended *cauda equina*, in essence a tail, which must be surgically removed at birth" (Marrs, 2013).

All of this brings us to another matter, one of highly controversial levels. There is a school of thought that believes—as a *direct* result of the tail controversy—that the Rh negatives have a genetic connection and lineage to the so-called Reptilians, those allegedly bipedal, lizard-like creatures, of otherworldly and menacing nature, that have become staple parts of UFO research, and conspiracy theorizing, and that may have some connection to the Anunnaki.

And it's not just physical differences that the Rh negatives display. It's one of a mind-based nature, too.

The Psychic Side of the Rh negatives

Regardless of what lies at the heart of the alien abduction controversy, the fact is that many abductees report that during the course of their abductions they were shown—by their dwarfish, gray-skinned captors—graphic imagery of the Earth of the future: a time filled with a decaying atmosphere, the collapse of the rainforests, the melting of the polar ice caps, and—well, the Armageddon-like visuals continue at a horrific, traumatic pace. Of those Rh negatives that have been polled, many have reported prophetic dreams. Others, without reporting abduction experiences, have suffered turbulent, deep-sleep visions of precisely the kinds of scenarios that alien abductees describe.

Other psychic phenomena are routinely and regularly reported by Rh negatives, including matters relative to what is termed *synchronicity*. In essence, a synchronicity can be termed a meaningful coincidence. Imagine thinking of a friend you have not seen nor spoken to for years. Within hours they phone you. That is a synchronicity. You're looking for a rare book and can't find a copy for sale anywhere. Days later, you find a copy casually discarded on a seat on the bus you take to work each morning. That is a synchronicity, too. It's a phenomenon that suggests our minds can influence—or, incredibly, even create—the reality around us. For the Rh negatives, synchronicities abound.

Extra-sensory perception (ESP) is high on the list of the amazing abilities of the Rh negatives, too. Mind-reading, telepathic communication, and psychic bonds with animals, are also all near the top of the list. A fascination—and very often a not-understood fascination—with astronomy, the domain of outer space, and the questions surrounding the existence of alien life occupy the minds of the Rh negatives. Perhaps most intriguing is that many Rh negatives feel that they have been pre-programmed to perform some specific task on the Earth—even though it's one they are unable to fully put their finger on and define. It's almost as if they are waiting to be "switched on," at which point everything will become crystal clear.

Negatives of the Powerful and Influential Variety

Coincidence or not, Rh negative blood abounds among both the famous and the infamous. President John F. Kennedy's alleged assassin, Lee Harvey Oswald, was Rh negative, as is his Russian wife, Marina. *The Investigation of the Assassination of President John*

F. Kennedy (more familiarly, but incorrectly, known as the "Warren Commission") quotes Marina as saying, after she became pregnant, to Lee: "...the doctors told me that I might lose the baby since I had Rh negative blood. Lee was very upset by this, but when he had his own blood checked, it turned out that he was also Rh negative. Only a very small percentage have Rh negative blood, and this very unusual coincidence—in which both husband and wife were Rh negative—pleased us very much" (*The Investigation of the Assassination of President John F. Kennedy: Performance of the Intelligence Agencies Book V Final Report*, 1976).

Rather amazingly, JFK himself was Rh negative, specifically AB negative. And Kennedy was far from being a solitary negative in the White House. President Dwight D. Eisenhower was O negative, as was President Richard Milhous Nixon. President Bill Clinton is AB Negative, and President George Bush, Sr., is A negative.

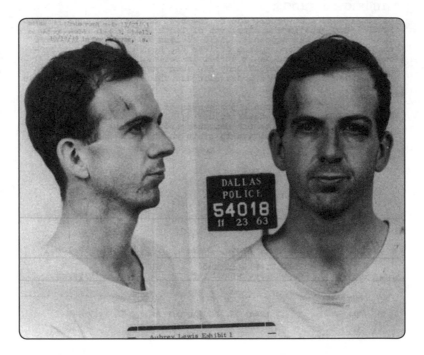

Lee Harvey Oswald, one of the world's most infamous Rh negatives.

Then there is the matter of the British royal family, which has a notable connection to the history of the U.S. presidential office, as David Icke observed: "If it really is the Land of the Free and if, as is claimed, anyone really can become the president, you would fairly expect that the 43 presidents from George Washington to George W. Bush would express that genetic diversity. You're having a laugh. The presidents of the United States are as much a royal dynasty as anything in Europe, from whence their bloodlines came" (Dubay, 2009).

And still on the issue of that Royal bloodline: Queen Elizabeth II, Prince Charles, and even William and Kate, are all Rh negative. What we have here, then, is a situation where some of the most powerful, influential, and famous figures in recent history are born out of the alien bloodline. Is this a case of the Anunnaki—no longer around on the scale they were hundreds of thousands of years ago—still ruling the Earth, but via a form of distant proxy? That may be exactly the situation. And while we're talking about blood...

A Bloody Controversy

If there is one thing, more than any other, central to the theme of this book, it's arguably not the Cro-Magnons, the Basques, the Rh negatives, or even extraterrestrial visitors. That central, binding issue is blood. And what is particularly fascinating about human blood is that the ancients didn't just recognized the importance of it when it came to well-being and health; they also had a keen awareness that there was a direct connection between blood and the gods—or the visiting aliens, depending on one's personal belief systems and ideologies.

Precisely why humankind of times long gone knew that blood and the gods were inextricably linked remains tantalizingly, and frustratingly, unknown. That ancient peoples did hold deep reverence for blood, however, and almost unanimously linked it to matters godlike, otherworldly, and paranormal is not a matter of any doubt, at all.

Aboriginal Beliefs and Blood

To demonstrate the sheer, widespread nature of how blood was revered in the distant past—and in some cases, still *is* revered in that very same fashion—we will begin with the aboriginal people of Australia. Their presence in Australia dates back some 70,000 years, when their descendants migrated there, from parts of Europe, Africa, and Asia. Within their culture, the aborigines, or aboriginal Australians, as they are also termed, have a god that is popularly known, when translated into English, as the Serpent Rainbow.

Ancient, aboriginal names for this particular god include Galeru, Numereji, and Wonungar—which are just three of many. The specific name of Serpent Rainbow, however, is a relatively recent one, created in the 20th century by a British anthropologist named Alfred Radcliffe-Brown. Despite the popularity of the English terminology, it's completely understandable as to why the aborigines prefer to use their tried and tested millennia-old names for this colorful entity: It helps them to continue to fly the flag of their culture. The name of this particular god is taken from its serpent-like, physical nature, coupled with its bright colors that provoke cascading, rainbow-style imagery.

Interestingly, the Serpent Rainbow is no lowly god. It is nothing less than a creator, a bringer of life, human or otherwise. In addition, the aborigines perceive the Serpent Rainbow was linked to none other than human blood. Rather notably, it's the female menstrual cycle that the Serpent Rainbow is so specifically connected to.

In other words, it is blood and the creation of life that the aborigines think of when it comes to the Serpent Rainbow—blood and the generation of life being integral parts of this story. On top of that, the Serpent Rainbow is credited with having brought into being a place called Arnhem Land. It's a near-40,000-square-mile area, located in Australia's Northern Territory. It is an area noted for one thing above all others: It is the home of the world's oldest stone axe, which is estimated to have been crafted around 35,000 years ago. This just happens to have been right around the historic period when Cro-Magnons were coming to the fore in Europe.

A blood-linked, supernatural deity, the generation of life, and matters relative to the precise same time frame in areas of the world that ultimately became France and Spain and home to the Cro-Magnons, are all key factors in the saga of the Serpent Rainbow of aboriginal teachings.

The Bible and Blood

For the life of the flesh is in the blood: and I have given it to you upon the altar to make an atonement for your souls: for it is the blood that maketh an atonement for the soul. Therefore I said unto the children of Israel, No soul of you shall eat blood, neither shall any stranger that sojourneth among you eat blood.... For it is the life of all flesh; the blood of it is for the life thereof: therefore I said unto the children of Israel, Ye shall eat the blood of no manner of flesh: for the life of all flesh is the blood thereof: whosoever eateth it shall be cut off ("Leviticus 17," 2015).

That is what we are told in Leviticus 17:11–14 in the pages of the Bible. Timothy S. Morton (who penned the paper "Power in the Blood?") says of this extract from the world's most famous book: "From this passage and those previous we can determine: Blood is the life of all flesh; God has given man blood for purposes of atonement; Blood can make atonement for the soul; Blood can speak to God; Eating blood could cost an Israelite his salvation" (Morton, 2015).

Acts 15:20 in the King James Version of the Bible includes the following, which adds weight to God's thundering displeasure of anyone who dared dine on blood: "That ye abstain from meats offered to idols, and from blood, and from things strangled, and from fornication: from which if ye keep yourselves, ye shall do well. Fare ye well" ("Acts 15:20").

On this matter, it's worth noting the story of the Seven Laws of Noah. Most people, whether they are a believer, a skeptic, or an atheist, have heard of the Ten Commandments, the rules provided to Moses by God on Mt. Sinai. Significantly fewer people possess an awareness of the Seven Laws of Noah, which are also referred to as the Noachide Laws. In English, the regulations translate as follows:

1. Do Not Deny God.

2. Do Not Blaspheme God.

3. Do Not Murder.

4. Do Not Engage in Incestuous, Adulterous or Homosexual Relationships.

5. Do Not Steal.

6. Do Not Eat of a Live Animal.

7. Establish Courts/Legal System to Ensure Law Obedience ("The Seven Noachide Laws," 2015).

Number six is of note because God was most determined to let everyone know that his almighty wrath would fall upon anyone who dared partake of blood. Again, we see evidence of the importance of blood and its links to a world famous deity. Not only that, it's a fact that references to blood absolutely dominate the pages of the Bible. Indeed, in the King James Bible, the word *blood* appears on almost 400 occasions, and most prolifically in the aforementioned Leviticus, where it surfaces on nearly 90 occasions.

Just like the Serpent Rainbow god of Australia, so the Christian god is an entity with significant ties to the matter of blood, and he is also a deity keenly aware of the priceless nature of blood, and why it should not be used recklessly and as a form of nourishment or as a sacrificial offering.

Blood Beliefs and the Pyramids

When most people think of pyramids, their minds are filled with imagery of the massive, mighty creations that dominate the landscape of Giza, Egypt. South America has no shortage of pyramids, however, particularly so in Peru's desert coast. Unlike the pyramids of Giza, their Peruvian counterparts are vastly and tragically under-explored, and our knowledge of the people that built these huge and impressive creations, including the Sechin pyramid, which has been conclusively shown—via carbon dating—to have been built around 1500 BC, is sorely lacking. There is something else, too: There is clear evidence that the Peruvians practiced human sacrifice at their pyramids, and definitely so at the Sechin pyramid, where a frieze provides eerie and unsettling imagery of just such a sacrifice taking place.

The Moche people of Peru, who lived in the vicinity of what today is the town of Trujillo, regularly engaged in human sacrifice, something that culminated with high priests drinking the blood of the dead from specifically crafted goblets.

The historical significance of blood.

Of most significance, consider the following: At the time Pachacuti Inca Yupanqui reigned in the Andes region known as the Kingdom of Cusco (a reign that lasted from 1438 to 1471), young children were sacrificed on an annual basis—specifically during the Winter Solstice. It was a bloody ritual called capacocha. Typically, the slaughtering occurred high in the mountainous areas of the region. Not only that, the Incas believed that the children—whose blood was drained from their bodies and drank by the elite—were returning to their original place of origin. And where might that have been? None other than the distant stars in the heavens above. As for the reason behind the sacrifices, it was a bizarre one: Pachacuti Inca believed he could harness and slow down the progress of time by slaughtering the young. Thus, we see, for the Incas, two things in particular: the importance of blood in trying to provoke a supernatural event (namely, reducing the speed at which time passes), and an acceptance that the universe around them was the original home of the sacrificed and the blood-drained.

On the aforementioned matter of the Winter Solstice, it's worth noting that Cro-Magnon man had a keen appreciation of the looming solstice and the drop in both temperature and food supplies that it offered. In his 1901 book, *History and Chronology of the Myth-Making Age*, J.F. Hewitt said that during the Paleolithic period, the Cro-Magnons "domesticated the reindeer, which furnished them with food, clothes and implements, and they had made the reindeer sun-god the ruler of their year. The dropping of his horns in autumn told them of the approach of winter, and their re-growth in spring heralded the coming summer. The prophet-god who spoke by these signs became the Celtic sun-god Cernunnos" (Hewitt, 1901).

The List Goes On

Then there are the Sun Dances of Native Americans, fearsome rituals in which young men have their chests pierced and are required to fast, and from whom significant amounts of blood are extracted and feasted upon—all of this to the rhythmic and near-hypnotic sounds of drums, to the presence of a blazing fire, and surrounding, sacred lands. The non-fatal sacrificing and blood-letting is undertaken to ensure that those partaking in the rituals will achieve their goals—which are usually to bring good fortune, health, and prosperity on the person's family.

What all of this tells us is that, regardless of the specific, geographic location under scrutiny, the ancients knew that human blood was somewhat different from, and more precious than, the body's organs, bones, muscle, and fat. Human blood was also perceived as having a connection to myriad numbers of gods—spanning from the Middle East to India, and from Australia to both the United States and South America.

Our distant ancestors knew something we have either lost or merely dismiss as folklore—namely, that blood and deities—or infinitely technologically superior extraterrestrials—were part and parcel of the very same phenomenon. That same phenomenon may have been born out of distorted tales—passed down, at first, orally, and later in written form—of how "the gods" performed miraculous changes to *Homo sapiens*, to the extent that their blood became more and more unique and godlike (Rh negative, in other words) than human. Hence the outrage exhibited by the gods when their unique cocktail of refined and distilled blood was spilled recklessly and used needlessly.

Rh Negatives and Inherited Memory

Is it feasible that some—or perhaps even all—Rh negatives have buried deep inside of their minds inherited memories of times and civilizations long gone, of the secret truths behind the extraterrestrial bloodline, and of who and what they *really* are? As we shall now see, that may very well be *exactly* what is going on, even if many of the Rh negatives may not be fully aware of the situation— aside, that is, from having a vague and unsettling sense of being somehow different to the rest of the human population. If such a theory has even a modicum of validity attached to it, then we should expect to see some form of manifestation of it in our world. *We do.* Two of the most prodigious researchers and writers on the mysteries of the distant past, extraterrestrial visitation thousands of years ago, and the overall "ancient aliens/astronauts" scenario are Rh negative.

Of course, those of a skeptical nature might be inclined to say that because a small percentage of the human race is Rh negative, then it stands to reason that a small percentage of authorities on ancient mysteries would be Rh negative, too. Such a scenario is hardly impossible, but it's worth noting that the two individuals I am referring are, arguably, the most visible and prolific writers on the enigmas surrounding human origins. What some might put down to random chance might very well be a case of ancient, ET-themed manipulation.

Chariots of the Negatives

There can be no doubt whatsoever that the most famous, and controversial, name within the field of ancient astronaut theorizing is that of Erich von Daniken. He just happens to be Rh negative. Swiss-born von Daniken was certainly not the first author to espouse that many of our ancient stories of gods coming down from the sky were actually distortions of alien visitations: W. Raymond Drake, Robert Charroux, and Morris Jessup wrote extensively on such matters years earlier. Von Daniken was, however, certainly the first person who elevated awareness of the subject to the general public on a massive scale. His 1968 book, *Chariots of the Gods?*, was a gigantic best-seller across the globe, and was followed up by numerous other titles, including *The Gold of the Gods, Signs of the Gods, The Return of the Gods*, and *Remnants of the Gods*.

It can accurately be said that without von Daniken's input, research into the ancient human-ET issue would not be on the scale that it is today. Could it be the case that von Daniken was unknowingly encoded, and therefore destined, to bring to the world a fantastic concept suggesting we (the human race) are the product of alien intervention? As we shall soon see, there is a very good reason why that just may be so.

Brad Steiger: An Rh Negative

Another famous author who also falls into the Rh negative category, and who has also written prodigiously on the matter of extraterrestrial-human interaction millennia ago, is Brad Steiger. Born in 1936 in Iowa, Steiger, while just a child, had a profound near-death experience that led him to gravitate toward Lutheranism, an arm of protestant Christianity. As with Erich von Daniken's, Steiger's books have captured the minds and imaginations of millions of people worldwide.

Among the many books that Steiger has written (which is in excess of 170) are more than a few that revolve around the many and varied enigmatic mysteries of the distant past. The list includes *Atlantis Rising, Mysteries of Time and Space, Worlds Before Our Own, Overlords of Atlantis and the Great Pyramids*, and *Super Scientists of Ancient Atlantis and Other Unknown Worlds*. Again, is it merely coincidence that—just like von Daniken, another Rh negative—Steiger has been instrumental in informing people on the many and varied enigmas surrounding ancient man?

The story does not end there, however. When Steiger's first wife became pregnant, there was deep concern that Steiger's Rh negative bloodline might be a matter of concern. It would have been, except for one thing: His wife turned out to be Rh negative, too. As is his sister, and as was his mother. In fact, the majority of Steiger's family is Rh negative.

Another Author and Another Rh negative

The late author Robert Anton Wilson was yet another influential figure and writer in the world of real-world enigmas who was Rh negative. And, in 1973, Wilson had a strange experience that had a direct link to the matter of none other than ancient aliens. He said:

On 23 July 1973, I had the impression that I was being contacted by some sort of advanced intellect from the system of the double star Sirius. On 23 July, ancient Egyptian priests began a series of rituals to Sirius, continuing until 8 September. Since Sirius is known as the "Dog Star", being in the constellation Canis Major, the period 23 July–8 September became known as "the dog days." On 23 July 1976, using a battery of yogic and shamanic techniques, I opened myself to another blast of Cosmic Wisdom and told the Transmitters that I wanted something objective this time around. The next week, *Time* magazine published a full-page review of Robert K.G. Temple's *The Sirius Mystery*, which claims that contact between Earth and Sirius occurred around 4500 BC in the Near East. The 23 July festivals in Egypt were part of Temple's evidence ("Robert Anton Wilson on Chaneling and ET Contact," 2011).

It's interesting to note that Wilson was someone who extensively researched, and wrote about, secret societies, influential elites, and manipulative power-mongers seeking to control and decide the fate of the world and future society. As this book demonstrates, the world of the elite is hardly Rh negative–free. But, if, certain Rh negative individuals, like Erich von Daniken, Brad Steiger, and Robert Anton Wilson, have been drawn to researching, and writing about, matters that are central to the story you are reading, how can that be the case? From where, or from whom, do they take their lead, their calling, and their inspiration? The answer takes us to a controversial realm, indeed: that of what is termed *inherited memory*.

Psychedelics and Ancient Imagery

A particularly potent fungus, one that can provoke remarkable, visionary-like experiences in an individual who partakes of it, *Amanita Muscaria* is also known as the sacred mushroom. It was back in the 1950s that one Andrija Puharich, an American of Yugoslavian extraction, delved deeply into the mind-altering abilities of this enigmatic fungus from his lab in Glen Cove, Maine. Puharich was someone who knew a great deal about how the mind could be manipulated: From 1953 to 1955, and as a captain in the U.S. Army, he was attached to the military's Army Chemical Center, Maryland. His work there spilled over into certain realms also being explored by the CIA, and ultimately became part and parcel of the work undertaken by the agency's "mind-control" program, MKUltra.

It turns out that Puharich had a fascination for the mysteries of ancient Egypt and was someone who came to believe that *Amantia Muscaria* allowed the participant's essence, or soul, to leave their body and, quite literally, to time-travel—in astral form—into the distant past. A theory that Puharich also addressed and that, in many ways, is even more thought-provoking suggested that rather than allowing the experiencer to travel into the very heart of millennia long gone, *Amantia Muscaria* actually provokes the surfacing of long-buried, encoded memories passed down from generation to generation, and possibly from time immemorial.

It so transpires that both scenarios fascinated the scientific elite and bigwigs of the CIA—to the extent that at some point in March 1956, an individual whose name is blacked out in the heavily redacted files that have been released via the Freedom of Information Act, was rendered into an altered state by *Amantia Muscaria* and monitored to determine the effects on the patient. Perhaps "on the guinea pig" would be a far better phrase to use. It transpires that the man—who was able to consciously recall the events after the effects wore off, and he duly shared them with the CIA's scientists—suddenly found himself plunged into the heart of ancient Egypt, where he saw nothing less than gleaming, extraterrestrial flying saucers levitating massive stone blocks into the air, and essentially, using a form of advanced anti-gravity to construct the pyramids in such a fashion.

The files reveal that the people attached to the project—which was a sub-project of the overall MKUltra umbrella—were in no less three minds as to what the experience told them. Some of the doctors and scientists believed that the man had experienced nothing but a vivid hallucination. Rather astonishingly, two of the team concluded that the man's soul had literally surfed time and stumbled on the secret of how the Pyramids at Giza, Egypt, were built. Then there was the theory that what the man experienced was none other than the spontaneous surfacing of deeply buried, inherited memories from times long gone that, for the most part remain latent and untapped, until something like *Amantia Muscaria* opens the door, so to speak.

With that said, let's now take a look at the concept of inherited memory and the way in which it might have played a role in influencing the likes of Brad Steiger, Erich von Daniken, and Robert Anton Wilson to gravitate to the very subjects that are relevant to the astounding story that this book tells.

The Mysteries of Memories Inherited

One of the most fascinating developments in this curious and not-well-understood phenomenon surfaced in December 2013. A research team from the department of psychiatry and behavioral sciences at Emory University School of Medicine (Atlanta, Georgia) published startling findings that added significant weight to the inherited memory theory. Brian G. Dias and Kerry J. Ressler, who penned the team's paper on the matter, "Parental Olfactory Experience Influences Behavior and Neural Structure in Subsequent Generations," revealed something extraordinary.

They undertook a study that was focused on exposing a group of mice to the odor of cherry blossom and taught the mice to associate the smell with looming, imminent danger. They then took a careful and close look at what changes—if any—this was having on the sperm of the male mice. It turns out there was a very important change: The mice DNA that was responsible for causing the sensitivity to the cherry blossom to occur, increased its activity within the sperm.

The next effect was on the brains of the mice, which led the team to say: "The experiences of a parent, even before conceiving, markedly influence both structure and function in the nervous system of subsequent generations" (Dias and Ressler, 2013).

This was proven when not just the direct offspring of the mice in question, but their "grandchildren," too, had all inherited this fear of cherry blossom, through the DNA of the parent mice. Dr. Dias said to the BBC: "This might be one mechanism that descendants show imprints of their ancestor. There is absolutely no doubt that what happens to the sperm and egg will affect subsequent generations" (Gallagher, 2013).

University College London's Professor Marcus Pembrey said of the findings of the Emory University School of Medicine that the conclusions had proven to be "highly relevant to phobias, anxiety and post-traumatic stress disorders," and demonstrated that the conclusions offered "compelling evidence" that, in one form or another, memory could be passed on throughout the generations. In this case, what we have is an inherited memory of a fear of one particular thing—in this case, the smell of cherry blossom. But, there is an even more amazing aspect to this controversy (Ibid.).

The Organ-Donor Affair

A number of people who have undergone organ transplant procedures have found themselves developing cravings for the kinds of foods that their donors were particularly fond of during the course of the donors' lives. There are more than 70 such examples on record, but, for our purposes, two will suffice.

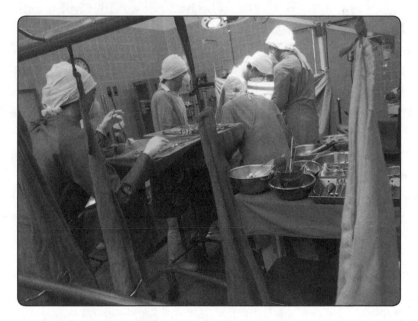

Ancient memories of Rh negatives.

In 2009, a 24-year-old Australian man from the city of Adelaide, named David Waters, received the heart of an 18-year-old donor of New South Wales, Kaden Delaney, who had been declared brain-dead after a violent car accident. In the wake of the successful transplant of Delaney's heart, Waters began to develop a sudden, out-of-the blue, craving for Burger Rings, which are Australia-based hamburger-flavored chips. Two years later, in 2011, the family of Delaney contacted Waters, just to see how he was doing and to determine if their son's heart had served a good, positive purpose, despite his tragic death. Waters was doing just fine. He got to know the Delaney family, and they exchanged e-mails, during which it was revealed Kaden Delaney had a particular taste for Burger Rings, eating at least one packet of them every single day—the very snack that Waters craved after his transplant.

Equally amazing, but filled with tragedy, is the story of an American man, Sonny Graham. In 1995, he received the heart of a victim of suicide, Terry Cottle, who had put a bullet in his brain. In the aftermath of the surgery, Graham met with Cottle's wife, Cheryl. It wasn't long before the pair fell in love and were soon married. It was a marriage not destined to last, however: In 2007, Sonny Graham shot himself in the throat. He did not survive.

What we have in the cases cited are examples of fear, food-based cravings, and suicidal tendencies being passed on from one living being to another—whether in mice or people, and whether by changes in sperm and DNA reactions, or by organ transplant. But, is it feasible that literal memories of the mind can be passed on from generation to generation?

Exploring the "Collective Unconscious"

One person who was a firm believer in just such a scenario was the renowned Swiss psychotherapist and psychiatrist Carl Gustav Jung. In referring to what he termed the *collective unconscious*, Jung said of his thesis:

> ...in addition to our immediate consciousness, which is of a thoroughly personal nature and which we believe to be the only empirical psyche (even if we tack on the personal unconscious as an appendix), there exists a second psychic system of a collective, universal, and impersonal nature which is identical in all individuals. This collective unconscious does

not develop individually but is inherited. It consists of pre-existent forms, the archetypes, which can only become conscious secondarily and which give definite form to certain psychic contents (Jung, 1981).

It's important to note that there are different kinds of memories. Episodic memories can include recalling when you last washed your car or the conversation you had yesterday with a colleague at work. Procedural memory is related to the ability to perform certain acts, after we have been taught how to do them, such as driving a car. Interestingly, procedural memory can be inherited—in both people and animals. The action of a dog circling the living room carpet several times before finally lying down and sleeping is a deeply buried memory of when, in times long gone, dogs lived in the wild and would flatten the grass to create a bed.

So far, there is no hard proof that literal, graphic memories can be inherited, to the extent that one can experience them in either a waking state or dream state—such as, for example, one's grandfather fighting against the Japanese, in the Pacific theater, post–Pearl Harbor, during the Second World War. There is, however, a wealth of material suggesting that Carl Jung was right on target with his collective unconscious theory—namely, that we all possess certain inherited traits.

With this in mind, it's not at all impossible that the Rh negatives, such as Brad Steiger, Robert Anton Wilson, and Erich von Daniken, were genetically encoded with some form of fragmentary memory that—even if it's not entirely clear or easy to pinpoint, categorize, and make sense of—let them know, or suspect, they are part of something bigger than the rest of the human race. It is, perhaps, something that sets them apart and something that drives them (even if they're not sure why), like a moth to a flame, to uncover the truths behind the key things that may have led to their very existence as Rh negatives in the first place: alien manipulation at a genetic, DNA level; and an extraterrestrial presence on Earth tens, or hundreds, of thousands of years ago.

· Conclusion ·

Having now dealt with the past and the present, there is really only one place left for us to head: the future. If, one day, confirmation is forthcoming that the Rh negatives are the product of deliberate alien intervention during the formative years of the human species, what might the response be? In all probability there wouldn't just be one, unified response, but an absolute multitude of reactions, most of them based around a collective, outright denial of the story. And there is a very good reason why millions—perhaps even *billions*—of people would maintain, and maintain strongly, that the revelation lacked merit.

Here's why: If the story of the Rh negatives does one thing more than any other, it does away with the need for a god, or multiple gods, to have played a role in the creation of the human race. Instead, the disclosure would demand that we have the existence of someone else's equivalent of NASA to thank for our very being. For entire swathes of the human population, such a suggestion would be complete anathema.

No one can deny that conflicting religious beliefs and teachings have been the cause of endless bloodshed, death, and outright warfare. In 2003, U.S. Army officer Lieutenant General William Boykin openly stated that the war on terror was nothing less than a battle with Satan. Then–Secretary of Defense Donald Rumsfeld flatly refused to criticize Boykin for his choice words. Nevertheless, Boykin was wrong: The war on terror was, and still is, a conflict with people—religious extremists and maniacs who believe that they are doing the work of their own brand of deity by crashing aircraft into buildings.

Also in 2003, intelligence briefings prepared for the White House by the Pentagon contained quotes on their covers that were taken from the epistles of Peter and the books of Psalms and Ephesians. One of them read: "Therefore put on the full armor of God, so that when the day of evil comes, you may be able to stand your ground, and after you have done everything, to stand" (Associated Press, 2009).

Then, in 2010, it was revealed that a firm in Michigan, Trijicon, had a $650 million contract to provide rifle sights to the U.S. Marine Corps. Rather incredibly, the sights were inscribed with biblical quotes—despite the fact that, by law, U.S. military law prohibits the proselytizing of any and all religions.

Moving on, we have the terrible tragedy of January 7, 2015, when Islamic terrorists shot and killed no fewer than 11 people and injured the same amount when they burst into the offices of the French newspaper *Charlie Hebdo*. The "crime" of those who lost their lives was that they dared to make biting, satirical comments about the Islamic religion. So, what does all of this have to do with the Rh negatives? The answer is *a lot*.

When the staff of a newspaper can be shot to death for daring to poke fun at Islam, and when a U.S. Army lieutenant general can state, without criticism from his superiors, that the war on terror is a conflict against the Devil himself, what we see is the sheer power that religious beliefs hold over people—whether crazed terrorists in France or a well-meaning officer in the U.S. military. And the Islamic and Christian religions are just two of *hundreds* that populate the planet. From the depths of the jungles of South America to the Eskimos of Canada, Alaska, and Greenland, and from the aborigines of Australia to Native American tribes, they all share two things in common: (1) They have beliefs in one or more deities, and (2) They deeply cherish those beliefs. And that's just the tip of the iceberg: There is not a single culture on the planet that lacks stories and traditions of an all-powerful, supernatural, supreme creator of God-like proportions.

Can you imagine what the reaction would be if, one day, an announcement was made—let's say via a combined committee comprised of senior personnel from the world's leading governments, scientific community, and the Vatican—stating that proof was now in hand, thanks to a careful study of the Rh negative phenomenon, that we 100 percent owe our origins not to an all-powerful god, but to ancient astronauts that created us as nothing more than a slave race to dutifully mine gold?

I strong suspect, and suggest, that most people would *not* be able to imagine what the reaction—in both the short term and the long term—would be. Certainly, the future would be a bleak one. If newspaper employees can be slaughtered for making a joke about Islam, then a statement to the effect that all worldwide religions are based on distorted legends, myths, and folklore of advanced extraterrestrials visiting the Earth in the distant past would, most likely, provoke social disorder on a scale barely conceivable. To say that chaos would erupt among both religious extremists and the average, everyday person who holds a religious belief, is an understatement.

If, in the god-fearing United States, it was revealed that the White House itself was backing the claims made concerning the Rh negatives, there would undoubtedly be demands—by millions—for the immediate removal of the president from the Oval Office.

No doubt, Middle Eastern lunatics would, step by step, take out their unbridled fury on just about anyone and everyone who dared to endorse the disclosure. And, for billions of people for whom religion and faith are the cornerstones of their very lives, we would likely see despair, depression, and perhaps even suicidal tendencies surface on a massive scale when faced with a world without a god and without a heaven, and without just about everything else that religion offers us—including some form of never ending life after this one.

For those very reasons, even if senior personnel within government office know—or, at the *very* least suspect—that everything said about the ET–Rh negative connection is true, it's most unlikely that we will ever receive ultimate confirmation. The ensuing psychological shock, worldwide, would likely be something from which billions of people might never recover. No government, regardless of what it knows—or thinks it knows—will ever risk such a situation occurring on a planetary scale.

And there is another issue in this saga of the impact that this entire controversy might have, to a worldwide degree: If, one day, it is proved that a small percentage of the human race is not entirely human after all, will we see a backlash against the Rh negatives? Will there be witch hunts? Could vigilante-style gangs roam the streets, seeking out those not-quite-humans? Might there be calls to have the negatives isolated from the rest of society—as in, for the rest of their lives? Could a form of "extraterrestrial racism"—born out of a fear that some of the negatives may be part of a sinister, alien agenda—develop both wildly and widely? Will we see the construction of countless "Extraterrestrial Guantanamo Bays"? Might just about everyone who has claimed an alien abduction event in their life, whether they are Rh negative or Rh positive, be taken into custody?

Such questions—and the attendant scenarios they provoke—might sound outlandish, but, almost certainly, they are not. We only have to take a look at the recent past to see that, if the world sees the truth, the Rh negatives will likely face futures of a very traumatic nature.

When, in the early to mid-1980s, the epidemic of acquired immunodeficiency syndrome exploded, there were calls for those with full-blown AIDS and those who were HIV positive to be placed into isolation. There was talk of quarantining the infected—forever. Doomsayers warned that the virus would escalate out of control, to the extent that it would spell the end of humanity. Others claimed that God was taking revenge on homosexuals because of their "sins." Even the Soviet Government's KGB got in on the act, spreading disinformation to try to frighten the American population. From a formerly classified U.S. Department of State document:

When the AIDS disease was first recognized in the early 1980s, its origins were a mystery. A deadly new disease had suddenly appeared, with no obvious explanation of what had caused it. In such a situation, false rumors and misinformation naturally arose, and Soviet disinformation specialists exploited this situation as well as the musings of conspiracy theorists to help shape their brief but highly effective disinformation campaign on this issue ("AIDS as a Biological Weapon," 2005).

The Department of State added:

In March, 1992, then-Russian intelligence chief, and later Russian Prime Minister Yevgeni Primakov, admitted that the disinformation service of the Soviet KGB had concocted the false story that the AIDS virus had been created in a U.S. military laboratory as a biological weapon.... The Soviets eventually abandoned the AIDS disinformation campaign under pressure from the U.S. Government in August 1987 (Ibid.).

It's intriguing—but also a matter of concern—that opposing nations might well exploit the Rh negative issue, in just such a fashion, and start spreading fabricated tales to scare the populace of whichever country they are currently in conflict with.

Bringing matters right up to the present day, few will forget the atmosphere of fear that gripped the American population in the latter part of 2014, when Ebola hemorrhagic fever surfaced in the United States—particularly so when people realized that, currently, there is no cure for Ebola. It all began in September 2014, when a Liberian man, Thomas Eric Duncan, who was visiting family in the Dallas, Texas, area, had the dubious honor of being the first person in the United States to show signs of what was suspected as being Ebola. On September 30th, the Centers for Disease Control confirmed what everyone was dreading: Duncan had Ebola. But not for long: He was dead by October 8th.

Three days later, one of Duncan's nurses at the Texas Health Presbyterian Hospital Dallas, at which he was treated, *also* fell sick with Ebola. Her name was Nina Pham. Seventy-two hours later, *another* nurse, Amber Joy Vinson, was also infected. Fortunately, both recovered. A physician named Craig Spencer, who had been involved in a project to help West Africans infected with Ebola, went down with the disease in New York. He, too, recovered. The nation, however, wondered where Ebola would erupt next. The answer: It didn't erupt anywhere. That was the beginning and the end of the 2014 Ebola outbreak: four cases confirmed in the United States. That's not quite the end of the story, however.

When the initial infection in Texas went from one, to two, and then to three, there were hysterical, nationwide calls for the city of Dallas to be quarantined, to be placed in lockdown, for martial law to be imposed to prevent the number of infected from spiraling out of control and spreading the virus across the rest of the Lone Star State, and, ultimately, all across America. It was like something out of the average zombie movie. Massive, unwarranted hysteria was running wildly out of control.

On Alex Jones's hugely popular Website, InfoWars, Paul Joseph Watson said: "Merely the suspicion of a limited Ebola outbreak in the United States would give the green light for federal authorities to seize draconian powers and detain Americans not even infected with the Ebola virus" (Watson, 2014).

On October 7, 2014, at the Intellihub site, Shepard Embellas wrote an article titled "Texas: Medical Martial Law and Forceful

Detention to Begin With Second 'Suspected' Patient." Its subtitle was: "Quarantine and Detention Camps to Become a Norm in America" (Ambellas, 2014).

Eight days later, the Before It's News Website ran an article on the Ebola outbreak in Dallas titled: "Get Ready for Public Health Emergency and Martial Law Restricting Travel—Dallas Creates Travel Disaster Declaration Over Ebola" (Before It's News, 2014).

As history has shown, martial law was not declared in Dallas, the city was not placed in unending lockdown mode, and no one was placed in detention camps. For a short time, however, shrill screams on the Internet succeeded in whipping up a frenzy, as well as a call for draconian laws to be introduced—as in, right now, before it's too late. All of this was caused by the medical plights of just four people—three of whom, it should not be forgotten, went on to make full, lasting recoveries.

Imagine, then, what the situation might be if it becomes clear to the populace that about 10 to 15 percent of all Americans are the product of something non-human. The U.S. population currently stands at about 322 million. Ten percent of that is 32 million. If just three people in Dallas, Texas, can wreak havoc and generate fear among the populace (and encouraged by a manipulative media), imagine the sheer chaos that could erupt should people be faced with the realization that there may well be more than *30 million Rh negatives in their midst.* Undoubtedly the ensuing anarchy, hysteria, fear, and maybe even lynch mobs that might follow would dwarf anything that came out of Dallas in 2014. And that's only America. It's not at all impossible that such a situation would be mirrored just about everywhere.

What does this mean for Rh negatives and positives alike? The answer is: It's all dependent on to what extent, if at all, the theory that the negatives are of an incredibly old, extraterrestrial bloodline takes hold. If it remains merely a theory, one followed by the con-spiracy-minded and UFO devotees alone, it's unlikely that we will ever see the sudden surfacing of a witch hunt of the negative variety.

Should, however, that situation change—and change radically—we may be in for deeply dark days. They may be days the likes of which have never been seen before: human pitted against human in violent, apocalyptic, anarchic battle, and all "thanks" to an incredibly old, space-faring civilization, its craving for gold, and its planet-wide re-programming of the genetic makeup of the human race in prehistory.

· Bibliography ·

"10th Planet Discovered." *http://science.nasa.gov/science-news/science-at-nasa/2005/29jul_planetx/.* July 29, 2005.

"Acts 15:20." *http://biblehub.com/kjv/acts/15.htm.* 2015.

"Acts 15:29." *http://biblehub.com/acts/15-29.htm.* 2014.

"AIDS as a Biological Weapon." *http://iipdigital.usembassy.gov/st/english/texttrans/2005/01/20050114151424tlahtnevel8. 222598e-02. html#axzz3SVOsgARz.* January 14, 2005.

Alford, Alan. *Gods of the New Millennium* (Southampton, UK: Eridu Books, 1996).

Allingham, William. "The Fairies." *www.sff.net/people/doylemacdonald/l_fairie.htm.* 2015.

Ambellas, Shepard. "Texas: Medical Martial Law and Forceful Detention to Begin With Second Suspected Patient." *www.intellihub.com/texas-medical-martial-law-forceful-detention-begin-second-suspected-patient/.* October 7, 2014.

"Amrita—Ambrosia—The Nectar of Immortality." *https://yogakinisis.wordpress.com/2013/05/14/amrita-ambrosia-the-nectar-of-immortality/.* May 14, 2013.

"Ancient Atomic Knowledge?" *www.bibliotecapleyades.net/ancientatomicwar/esp_ancient_atomic_10.htm.* 2015.

"Antediluvian World, The." *ww.earthhistory.org.uk/before-the-cataclysm/before-the-flood.* 2015.

Aquinas, Thomas. *Basic Writings of St. Thomas Aquinas: (Volume 1)* (Indianapolis, Ind.: Hackett Publishing Company, Inc., 1997).

Arnold, Thomas. *The History of Rome* (Ann Arbor, Mich.: Michigan Publishing, 2006).

"Artificial Wombs." *www.mhhe.com/biosci/genbio/olc_linkedcontent/ bioethics_cases/g-bioe-17.htm.* 2000.

Associated Press. "Pentagon Ends Use of Bibles in Pentagon Briefings." *http://nypost.com/2009/05/19/pentagon-ends-use-of-bibles-in-briefings/.* May 19, 2009.

"Basque." *www.britannica.com/EBchecked/topic/55335/Basque.* June 10, 2014.

Before It's News. "Get Ready for Public Health Emergency and Martial Law Restricting Travel, Dallas Creates Travel Disaster Declaration Over Ebola." *http://beforeitsnews.com/ alternative/2014/10/get-ready-for-public-health-emergency-and-martial-law-restrictng-travel-dallas-declares-travel-disaster-declaration-over-ebola-picture-3045744.html.* October 15, 2014.

Behar, Doron M. "The Basque Paradigm: Genetic Evidence of a Maternal Continuity in the Franco-Cantabrian Region since Pre-Neolithic Times." *www.ncbi.nlm.nih.gov/pmc/articles/ PMC3309182/.* March 9, 2012.

Bell, Art, and Whitley Strieber. *The Coming Global Superstorm* (New York: Pocket, 2004).

Bethurum, Truman. *Aboard a Flying Saucer)*Los Angeles, Calif.: DeVorss & Co., 1954).

"Bioethics: Human-Animal Hybrid Embryos." *www.bbc.co.uk/ethics/ animals/using/hybridembryos_1.shtml.* 2014.

Bishop, Greg. *Project Beta* (New York: Paraview-Pocket Books, 2005).

"Blood Test for Rh Status and Antibody Screen." *www.babycenter. com/0_blood-test-for-rh-status-and-antibody-screen_1480.bc.* 2015.

Blum, Ralph, and Judy Blum. *Beyond Earth* (New York: Bantam Books, 1978).

Brinkmann, Susan. "UK Scientists Secretly Create 155 Human-Animal Hybrids." *www.womenofgrace.com/blog/?p=8699.* July 25, 2011.

"British Lab Admits of Morphing Humans and Animals Into Hybrids." *http://macedoniaonline.eu/content/view/18719/56/.* July 26, 2011.

Bronznick, Norman, with David Stern and Mark Jay Mirsky (translators). "The Story of Lilith the Alphabet of ben Sira Question #5 (23a-b)." *http://jewishchristianlit.com/Topics/Lilith/ alphabet.html.* 2015.

Carpenter, John. "Abduction Notes." *MUFON UFO Journal*, April 1993.

Carus, Dr. Paul. *History of the Devil and the Idea of Evil* (Whitefish, Mont.: Kessinger Publishing, LLC, 2004).

Central Intelligence Agency. "FLYING SAUCERS OVER BELGIAN CONGO URANIUM MINES." August 16, 1952. Declassified under the terms of the Freedom of Information Act.

Chambers, Dr. Paul. *Sex and the Paranormal* (London: Blandford, 1999).

"Changelings and Fairy Babies." *https://myndandmist.wordpress. com/2012/06/24/changelings-and-fairy-babies/.* June 24, 2012.

"Charlie Hebdo" *www.theguardian.com/media/charlie-hebdo.* 2015.

Choi, Charles Q. "Humans Did Not Wipe Out the Neanderthals, New Research Suggests." *www.livescience.com/47460-neanderthal-extinction-revealed.html.* August 20, 2014.

Clark, Gerald R. *The Anunnaki of Nibiru* (CreateSpace Independent Publishing Platform, 2013).

Clelland, Mike. "I Have Rh Negative Blood." *http://hiddenexperience. blogspot.com/2012/03/i-have-rh-negative-blood.html.* March 29, 2012.

———. "Owls and the Abductee." *http://hiddenexperience.blogspot. com/2013/07/owls-and-ufo-abductee.html.* July 3, 2013.

Collins, Nick. "Ethical Rules Needed to Curb 'Frankenstein-Like Experiments' on Animals." *www.telegraph.co.uk/news/science/ science-news/8652093/Ethical-rules-needed-to-curb-Frankenstein-like-experiments-on-animals.html.* July 22, 2011.

"Complete Solar System of 12 Celestial Bodies, The." *www. mesopotamiangods.com/the-complete-solar-system-of-12-celestial-bodies/.* 2015.

Connor, Steve. "The Neanderthal Murder Mystery." *www.independent. co.uk/news/science/the-neanderthal-murder-mystery-888276.html.* August 8, 2008.

Conroy, Ed. *Report on Communion* (New York: Avon Books, 1989).

Corso, Philip J., with William J. Birnes. *The Day After Roswell* (New York: Simon & Schuster, 1997).

Creighton, Gordon. "The Amazing Case of Antonio Villas Boas." *The Humanoids*, edited by Charles Bowen (Chicago, Ill.: Henry Regency Company, 1969).

"Cro-Magnon." *www.britannica.com/EBchecked/topic/143532/Cro-Magnon.* 2015.

"Cro-Magnon." *www.netlibrary.net/articles/cro-magnon.* 2015.

"Cro-Magnon 1." *http://humanorigins.si.edu/evidence/human-fossils/fossils/cro-magnon-1*. 2015.

De Ugalde, Martin. "A Short History of the Basque Country." *www.buber.net/Basque/History/shorthist.html*. 2015.

Deems, James M. "The Hidden Treasure of Lascaux Cave." *www.jamesmdeem.com/stories.cave3.html*. 2014.

Dias, Brian G., and Kerry J. Ressler. "Parental Olfactory Experience Influences Behavior and Neural Structure in Subsequent Generations." *www.nature.com/neuro/journal/v17/n1/full/nn.3594.html*. December 1, 2013.

Diaz, Frank. *The Gospel of the Toltecs: The Life and Teachings of Quetzalcoatl* (Rochester, Vt.: Bear & Co., 2002).

Donnelly, Ignatius. *Atlantis: The Antediluvian World* (Whitefish, Mont.: Kessinger Publishing, LLC, 2010).

Dr. Intimacy. "Incubus and Succubus Sex Demons of the Night." *https://drintimacy.wordpress.com/incubus-and-succubus-sex-demons-of-the-night/*. 2015.

"Dr. Leir's Bio." *www.alienscalpel.com/dr-leirs-bio*. May 11, 2010.

Dubay, Eric. *The Atlantean Conspiracy* (Raleigh, N.C.: Lulu, 2009).

Eck, Jason C. "Cauda Equina Syndrome." *www.emedicinehealth.com/cauda_equina_syndrome/article_em.htm*. 2015.

Editors of Encyclopedia Britannica. "Quetzalcoatl." *www.britannica.com/EBchecked/topic/487168/Quetzalcoatl*. August 26, 2014.

"Enki and Ninhursag." *www.gatewaystobabylon.com/myths/texts/retellings/enkininhur.htm*. 2015.

"Epic of Gilgamesh—Sumerian Flood Story 2750–2500 BCE." *www.historywiz.com/primarysources/sumerianflood.html*. 2015.

"Epic of Gilgamesh, The." *www.sparknotes.com/lit/gilgamesh/section9.rhtml*. 2015.

Evans-Wentz, W.Y. *The Fairy Faith in Celtic Countries* Pompton Plains, N.J.: New Page Books, 2004).

"Faerie Folklore in Medieval Tales—An Introduction." *www.academia.edu/300335/Faerie_Folklore_in_Medieval_Tales_an_Introduction*. 2015.

Fawcett, Lawrence, and Barry J. Greenwood. *Clear Intent* (Englewood Cliffs, N.J.: Prentice-Hall, Inc., 1984).

Forbes, Peter. "Neanderthal Man: In Search of Lost Genomes by Svante Paabo—Review." *www.theguardian.com/books/2014/feb/19/neanderthal-man-search-lost-genomes- svante-paabo*. February 20, 2014.

Fowler, Raymond E. *The Andreasson Affair* (Englewood Cliffs, N.J.: Prentice-Hall, 1979).

———. *The Andreasson Legacy* (New York: Marlowe & Co., 1997).

Friedman, Stanton T., and Kathleen Marden. *Captured! The Betty and Barney Hill UFO Experience* (Pompton Plains, N.J.: 2007).

Fuller, John G. *The Interrupted Journey* (New York: The Dial Press, 1965).

Gallagher, James. "'Memories' Pass Between Generations." *www.bbc.com/news/health-25156510*. December 1, 2013.

Gardner, Lawrence. *Genesis of the Grail Kings* (New York: Bantam Press, 1999).

Gardner, M.B., and P.A. Luciw. "Macaque Models of Human Infectious Disease." *www.ncbi.nlm.nih.gov/pubmed/18323583*. 2008.

Gary. "From Cauldron to Grail in Celtic Mythology." *http://celticmythpodshow.com/blog/from-cauldron-to-grail-in-celtic-mytholgy/*. March 3, 2013.

"Genes Link Celts to Basques." *http://news.bbc.co.uk/2/hi/uk_news/wales/1256894.stm*. April 3, 2001.

"Genesis 1." *http://biblehub.com/niv/genesis/1.htm*. 2013.

"Genesis 2:18–25." *http://biblia.com/bible/esv/Ge%202.18-25*. 2015.

"Genesis 6:2." *http://biblehub.com/genesis/6-2.htm*. 2013.

"Genesis 19." *http://biblehub.com/niv/genesis/19.htm*. 2013.

"Genetics Helps Scientists Determine Basque Origins." *http://raceandhistory.com/worldhotspots/basque.htm*. 2009.

"Great Flood: The Epic of Atrahatis, The." *www.livius.org/fa-fn/flood/flood3-t-atrahasis.html*. 2015.

"Great Gods of the Celts: Manannan mac Lir." *http://manannan.net/library/comparative.html*. 2015.

Harding, Anthony J. "A Brief History of Blood Transfusion." *www.ibms.org/go/nm:history-blood-transfusion*. November 2005.

Hardy, Chris H. *DNA of the Gods: The Anunnaki Creation of Eve and the Alien Battle for Humanity* (Rochester, Vt.: Bear & Company, 2014).

"Heart Rate Training." *www.ntcceagles.com/index.php?module=Pagesetter&func=viewpub&tid=18&pid=41*. 2015.

"Heart Transplant Man Dies Like Suicide Donor." *www.telegraph.co.uk/news/worldnews/1584248/Heart-transplant-man-dies-like-suicide-donor.html*. April 7, 2008.

Hewitt, J.F. *History and Chronology of the Myth-Making Age* (London: Parker & Co., 1901).

Hickson, Charles, and William Mendez. *UFO Contact at Pascagoula* (Phoenix, Ariz.: Wendel C. Stevens Publishing, 1983).

"History of Blood Transfusion." *www.redcrossblood.org/learn-about-blood/history-blood-transfusion*. 2015.

Hogarth, Donald D. "Robert Rich Sharp (1881–1960), Discoverer of the Shinkolobwe Radium–Uranium Orebodies." *www.maneyonline. com/doi/abs/10.1179/0082288414Z.00000000029*. Maney Online, Volume 46, Issue 1, April 2014.

"Homo Neanderthalensis." *http://humanorigins.si.edu/evidence/human-fossils/species/homo-neanderthalensis*. 2015.

Hopkins, Budd. *Art, Life and UFOs: A Memoir* (San Antonio, Tex.: Anomalist Books, 2009).

———. *Intruders: The Incredible Visitations at Copley Woods* (New York: Random House, 1987).

———. *Missing Time* (New York: Ballantine Books, 1981).

"Hypertension/High Blood Pressure Health Center." *www.webmd. com/hypertension-high-blood-pressure/*. 2015.

"Hypnagogia and Sleep Paralysis." *www.sleepdex.org/hypnogogia. htm*. 2015.

Inglis-Arkell, Esther. "The Science of Human Tails." *http://io9. com/5967742/the-science-of-human-tails*. December 12, 2012.

Innes, Emma. "Indian Teenager Is Worshipped Because He Has a Seven Inch TAIL—but May Need it Removed as He's Unable to Walk." *www.dailymail.co.uk/health/article-2660148/Indian-teenager-worshipped-seven-inch-TAIL-need-removed-hes-unable-walk.html*. June 17, 2014.

"Introducing Gilgamesh." *www.bcconline.com/huma5/gilgamesh. htm*. 2015.

Investigation of the Assassination of President John F. Kennedy: Performance of the Intelligence Agencies Book V Final Report, The (Washington, D.C.: U.S. Government Printing Office, 1976).

"Isaiah Chapter 34." [BEGIN]*http://lantius.org/leew/project/bible/ isaiah/isaiah34.htm/*. December 9, 2002.

"Isaiah Chapter 34." *www.usccb.org/bible/isaiah/34*. 2015.

Jacobs, David M. *The Threat: Revealing the Secret Alien Agenda* (New York: Fireside, 1999).

Jha, Alok. "Obama Climate Adviser Open to Geo-Engineering to Tackle Global Warming." *www.theguardian.com/ environment/2009/apr/08/geo-engineering-john-holdren*. April 8, 2009.

"John 6:50." *http://biblehub.com/john/6-50.htm*. 2015.

"John Wyndham." *www.theguardian.com/books/2008/jun/10/ johnwyndham*. July 22, 2008.

"Joseph McCabe." *http://onlinebooks.library.upenn.edu/webbin/book/ lookupname?key=McCabe%2C%20Joseph%2C%201867-1955*. 2015.

Jung, C.G. *The Archetypes and the Collective Unconscious* (Princeton, N.J.: Princeton University Press, 1981).

"Karl Landsteiner (1868–1943)." *www.rockefeller.edu/about/awards/lasker/ klandsteiner*. 2015.

Keefe, Rick. "ET Beings From Korendor." *www.ufohypotheses.com/ korendor.htm*. February 26, 2012.

Keel, John. *Our Haunted Planet* (Point Pleasant, W.V.: New Saucerian Books, 2014).

Klass, Philip J. *The Skeptics UFO Newsletter*, Vol. 32. www.csicop.org/ specialarticles/show/klass_files_volume_32/. March 1, 1995.

Kurlansky, Mark. *The Basque History of the World* (London: Penguin Books, 2001).

"LA Jazz Singer's Book Deal to Reveal Her Sex Life With Aliens." *www.reptilianagenda.com/exp/e100799a.shtml*. June 8, 1998.

Lacaux, Nathalie. "The Brain of Cro-Magnon Versus Modern Man: A Matter of Size." *www.inria.fr/en/centre/rennes/news/cro-magnon-vs-modern-man*. January 26, 2011.

Lammer, Dr. Helmout, and Marion Lammer. *MILABS: Military Mind Control & Alien Abduction* (Lilburn, Ga.: IllumiNet Press, 1999).

"Leviticus 17." *http://biblehub.com/niv/leviticus/17.htm*. 2015.

"Lilith." *http://jewishchristianlit.com/Topics/Lilith/*. 2015.

"Lilith Myth, The." *http://gnosis.org/lilith.htm*. 2015.

Lindemans, Micha F. "Ninhursag." *www.pantheon.org/articles/n/ ninhursag.html*. June 21, 1997.

Mack, John E. *Abduction: Human Encounters With Aliens* (New York: Ballantine Books, 1994).

———. *Passport to the Cosmos* (New York: Three Rivers Press, 1999).

MacQuarrie, Kim. "Why the Incas Offered Up Child Sacrifices." *www. theguardian.com/science/2013/aug/04/why-incas-performed-human-sacrifice*. August 3, 2013.

Marrs, Jim. *Our Occulted History* (New York: HarperCollins Publishers, 2013).

Martinez, Krystina. "Ebola in Dallas: A Timeline." *http://keranews.org/ post/ebola-dallas-timeline*. November 7, 2014.

Martinez, Susan B. *The Mysterious Origins of Hybrid Man: Crossbreeding and the Unexpected Family Tree of Humanity* (Rochester, Vt.: Bear & Company, 2013).

McAuliffe, Kathleen. "If Modern Humans Are So Smart, Why Are Our Brains Shrinking?" *http://discovermagazine.com/2010/sep/25-modern-humans-smart-why-brain-shrinking.* January 20, 2011.

McCabe, Joseph. *The Story of Religious Controversy* (Boston, Mass.: Stratford Company, 1929).

"Megabeasts' Sudden Death." *http://amser.org/index.php?P=AMSER--ResourceFrame&resourceId=10794.* 2015.

Mejia, Paula. "Fetuses in Artificial Wombs: Medical Marvel or Misogynist Malpractice?" *www.newsweek.com/fetuses-artificial-wombs-medical-marvel-or-misogynist-malpractice-263308.* August 6, 2014.

"Mining Concessions in Panama." *http://en.centralamericadata.com/en/search?q1=content_en_le%3A%22Mining+concessions%22&q2=mattersInCountry_en_le%3A%22Panama%22.* 2015.

Mitchell, Stephen. *Gilgamesh: A New English Version* (New York: Atria Books, 2006).

Morton, Timothy S. "Power in the Blood?" *www.preservedwords.com/blood-pv.htm.* 2015.

"Myth of Manannan Mac Lir, The." *www.isleofman.com/welcome/mythology-and-folklore/manannan-mac-lir/.* 2015.

Ness, R.C. "The Old Hag Phenomenon as Sleep Paralysis: A Biocultural Interpretation." *www.ncbi.nlm.nih.gov/pubmed/699620.* March, 1978.

Nichols, Kenneth D. *The Road to Trinity* (New York: Morrow, 1987).

"Ninhursag." *www.britannica.com/EBchecked/topic/415736/Ninhursag.* 2015.

"No Fix for 'Jesus Rifles' Deploying to Afghanistan." *http://usnews.nbcnews.com/_news/2012/09/26/14112808-no-fix-for-jesus-rifles-deploying-to-afghanistan?lite.* September 26, 2012.

Norman, Jeremy. "Discovery of the Cro-Magnons, the First European Early Modern Humans (Circa 41,000 BCE)." *www.historyofinformation.com/expanded.php?id=4057.* 2015.

"O-Negative Blood Group." *www.md-health.com/O-Negative-Blood-Group.html.* February 19, 2015.

O'Ehley, James. "Village of the Damned." *www.scifimoviepage.com/villageof.html.* 1997.

Okie, Susan. "Mammoth Extinction Mystery Draws 3 Theories." *www. arn.org/docs2/news/mammothextinction112201.htm.* November 22, 2001.

Oppenheimer, Stephen. *The Origins of the British* (London: Robinson Publishing, 2007).

Orozko, Chela. "The Legend of Quetzalcoatl." *www.inside-mexico.com/ the-legend-of-quetzalcoatl-by-chela-orozco/.* September 30, 2013.

"Psalm 78:24." *http://biblehub.com/psalms/78-24.htm.* 2015.

Puharich, Andrija. *The Sacred Mushroom* (New York: Doubleday & Company, Inc., 1959).

Pye, Lloyd. *Everything You Know Is Wrong* (Madeira Beach, Fla.: Adamu Press, 1997).

"Quinn's Story...Profile of an Abductee." *www.pararesearchers.org/ index.php?/20080804508/Alien-Contact-Abduction/Quinn-s-Story. html.* 1992.

"Rainbow Serpent, The." *https://www.aboriginalartonline.com/culture/ rainbow.php.* 2001.

Redd, Nola Taylor. "Did a Comet Really Chill and Kill Clovis Culture?" *www.livescience.com/27565-did-comet-kill-clovis-culture. html.* February 28, 2013.

Redfern, Nick. Interview with Alison, December 3, 2014.

———. Interview with Annika, January 14, 2015.

———. Interview with Brenda, August 24, 2014.

———. Interview with Jennifer, June 18, 2011.

———. Interview with Liz, May 28, 2013.

———. "Pancakes From the Stars." *http://mysteriousuniverse. org/2015/01/pancakes-from-the-stars/.* January 29, 2015.

———. *The Pyramids and the Pentagon* (Pompton Plains, N.J.: New Page Books 2012).

———. *The Real Men in Black* (Pompton Plains, N.J.: New Page Books, 2011).

"Repairing the Ozone Layer." *http://yosemite.epa.gov/R10/airpage.nsf/ webpage/Repairing+The+Ozone+Layer.* 2015.

"Rh Disease." *www.marchofdimes.org/baby/rh-disease.aspx#.* December 2009.

"Rh Factor." *http://americanpregnancy.org/pregnancy-complications/ rh-factor/.* 2015.

"Rh Factor: Enhancing the Safety of Blood Transfusion and Setting the Stage for Preventing Hemolytic Disease of the Newborn, The." *http://centennial.rucares.org/index.php?page=Rh_Factor*. 2015.

"Rh-negative Celebrities." *http://rhesusnegativity.blogspot.com/2012/03/rh-negative-celebrities.html*. March 22, 2012.

"Robert Anton Wilson on Chaneling and ET Contact." *http://dogtraininginsight.com/how-to-train-my-dog/robert-anton-wilson-on-channeling-and-et-contact/*. August 30, 2011.

Rosemary's Baby (1968). *www.filmsite.org/rosem.html*. 2015.

Royce, Mabel. "Blood of the Gods." *www.rhnegativeregistry.com/blood-of-the-gods-by-mabel-royce.html*. 1976.

Rudd, Steve. "The Epic of Gilgamesh." *www.noahs-ark.tv/noahs-ark-flood-creation-stories-myths-epic-of-gilgamesh-neo-babylonian-akkadian-cuneiform-ut-napistim-tablet11-1150bc.htm*. 2015.

Sabrina. "Cymidei Cymeinfoll." *www.goddessaday.com/western-european/cymidei-cymeinfoll*. June 9, 2008.

Schwarz, Rob. "The Old Hag Syndrome." *www.strangerdimensions.com/2011/10/13/the-old-hag-syndrome/*. October 13, 2011.

"Seven Noachide Laws, The." *www.jewishvirtuallibrary.org/jsource/Judaism/The_Seven_Noahide_Laws.html*. 2015.

Shears, Richard. "Do Hearts Have Memories? Transplant Patient Gets Craving for Food Eaten by Organ Donor." *www.dailymail.co.uk/news/article-1237998/Heart-transplant-patient-gets-craving-food-eaten-organ-donor.html*. December 23, 2009.

Simpson, Joe. "The Man who Found Broighter Gold." *www.bbc.co.uk/northernireland/yourplaceandmine/londonderry/broighter_gold_simpson.htm*. May 2006.

Sitchin, Zecharia. *Divine Encounters* (New York: Avon Books, 1995).

———. *Genesis Revisited* (New York: Avon Books, 1990).

———. *The Cosmic Code* (New York: Avon Books, 1998).

———. *The Lost Realms* (New York: Avon Books, 1990).

———. *The 12th Planet* (New York: HarperCollins, 2007).

———. *When Time Began* (New York: Avon Books, 1993).

Sterling, Robert. "Lustful Exploits With Scale-skinned Lizard Lovers." *The Excluded Middle*, No. 9, Winter 1999.

Stonebrooke, Pamela. Open letter, 1998 (undated).

Strieber, Whitley. *Communion* (New York: William Morrow & Co., 1987).

———. *Transformation* (New York: William Morrow & Co., 1988).

————. "Friends & Fellow UFO Experiencers." *www.unknowncountry.com/insight/friends-fellow-ufo-experiencers*. June 22, 2004.

Summers, Montague (translator), Heinrich Kramer, and James Sprenger (authors). *Malleus Maleficarum* (CreateSpace Independent Publishing Platform, 2013).

"Sun Dance." *www.native-americans-online.com/native-american-sun-dance.html*. 2014.

Szalay, Jessie. "Neanderthals: Facts About Our Extinct Human Relatives." *www.livescience.com/28036-neanderthals-facts-about-our-extinct-human-relatives.html*. March 19, 2013.

Tellinger, Michael. *African Temples of the Anunnaki* (Rochester, Vt.: Bear & Company, 2013).

————. *Slave Species of the Gods* (Rochester, Vt.: Bear & Company, 2012).

Thomas, Jr., Robert McG. "Marcel Radidat Is Dead at 72; Found Lascaux Cave Paintings." *www.nytimes.com/1995/03/31/obituaries/marcel-ravidat-is-dead-at-72-found-lascaux-cave-paintings.html*. March 31, 1995.

"Thomas the Rhymer and the Queen of Elfland." *http://myths.e2bn.org/mythsandlegends/origins530-thomas-the-rhymer-and-the-queen-of-elfland.html*. 2006.

Thompson, Reginald C. *Devils and Evil Spirits of Babylonia* (Whitefish, Mont.: Kessinger Publishing, 2003).

"Thoracic Outlet Syndrome." *www.nlm.nih.gov/medlineplus/thoracicoutletsyndrome.html*. August 12, 2014.

Thornhill, Ted. "Neanderthals Beat Modern Humans to the Seas by 50,000 Years, Say Scientists." *www.dailymail.co.uk/sciencetech/article-2108651/Neanderthals-beat-modern-humans-seas-50-000-years-say-scientists.html*. March 1, 2012.

Tonnies, Mac. *The Cryptoterrestrials* (San Antonio, Tex.: Anomalist Books, 2010).

Turner, Karla. *Into the Fringe* (New York: Berkley Books, 1992).

United States Geological Survey, 2002 Mineral Industry Report. Washington, D.C.: U.S. Government Printing Office, 2007.

"US Is 'Battling Satan' Says General." *http://news.bbc.co.uk/2/hi/americas/3199212.stm*. October 17, 2003.

Vergano, Dan. "New Clues About Human Sacrifices at Ancient Peruvian Temple." *http://news.nationalgeographic.com/news/2013/11/131119-moche-human-sacrifice-war-victims-burials-archaeology-science/*. November 19, 2013.

Verkuilen, Pamela E. "Spinal Abnormalities Rarely Cause Back Problems." *www.spine-health.com/conditions/spine-anatomy/spinal-abnormalities-rarely-cause-back-problems.* November 18, 2005.

Villas Boas, Antonio. Deposition, February 22, 1958.

Von Ward, Paul. *We've Never Been Alone* (Newburyport, Mass.: Hampton Roads, 2011).

Wagner, Thomas M. "The Midwich Cuckoos." *www.sfreviews.net/midwich.html.* 2004.

Walton, Travis. *Fire in the Sky* (New York: Marlowe & Co., 1997).

Watson, Paul Joseph. "Ebola: Medical Martial Law? Mere Suspicion of Outbreak Could Spark Panic." *www.infowars.com/ebola-medical-martial-law/.* August 1, 2014.

"We Cannot Let DRC Fail." *www.southerntimesafrica.com/news_article.php?id=6419&type=81#.VOY5ku85Cpo.* 2015.

Weatherly, David. *The Black Eyed Children* (Ariz.: Leprechaun Press, 2012).

Weber, Mark. "Israel Is Developing 'Ethnic Bomb' for Growing Biological Weapons Arsenal." *The Journal of Historical Review* (Vol. 17, No. 6), pages 24–25. November–December 1998.

Webster, Wentworth. *Basque Legends* (London: Griffin & Farran, 1877).

"What Is My Rhesus Status, and How Will it Affect My Pregnancy?" *www.babycentre.co.uk/a568837/what-is-my-rhesus-status-and-how-will-it-affect-my-pregnancy.* September 2012.

"What Lurks in the Outer Solar System?" *http://science.nasa.gov/science-news/science-at-nasa/2001/ast13sep_1/.* September 13, 2001.

"White Powder of Gold (ORME)." *www.tokenrock.com/explain-white-powder-of-gold--orme--84.html.* 2010.

Whitehouse, Dr. David. "Oldest Lunar Calendar Identified." *http://news.bbc.co.uk/2/hi/science/nature/975360.stm.* October 16, 2000.

"Who Discovered the Neanderthals?" *http://discovery.yukozimo.com/who-discovered-the-neanderthals/.* 2015.

"Who Is Manannan Mac Lir?" *http://manannan.net/whois/index.html.* 2015.

"Who Made the Neanderthal Flute?" *www.greenwych.ca/divje-b.htm.* November 2006.

Wilde, F.S. *Ancient Legends of Ireland* (New York: Sterling, 1992).

Wildon, Katharina. "Eye of the Storm: Interview With Lisa." *www.karlaturner.org/articles/related/eye-of-the-storm.html.* 2008.

Witcombe, Christopher, L.C.E. "Eve and Lilith." *http://witcombe.sbc.edu/ eve-women/7evelilith.html*. 2000.

Woo, Dr. Joseph. "A Short History of Amniocentesis, Fetoscopy and Chorionic Villus Sampling." *www.ob-ultrasound.net/amniocentesis. html*. 2015.

Zyga, Lisa. "Cro Magnon Skull Shows That Our Brains Have Shrunk." *http://phys.org/news187877156.html*. March 15, 2010.

· Index ·

· About the Author ·

NICK REDFERN is the author of more than 30 books on UFOs, Bigfoot, lake monsters, the Abominable Snowman, and Hollywood scandals, including *Monster Files, Memoirs of a Monster Hunter, The Real Men in Black, The NASA Conspiracies, Keep Out!, The Pyramids and the Pentagon, Contactees, The World's Weirdest Places, For Nobody's Eyes Only,* and *Close Encounters of the Fatal Kind.* He has appeared on more than 70 TV shows, including Fox News; the BBC's *Out of This World;* the SyFy Channel's *Proof Positive;* the Space Channel's *Fields of Fear;* the History Channel's *Monster Quest, America's Book of Secrets, Ancient Aliens,* and *UFO Hunters;* Science's *The Unexplained Files;* the National Geographic Channel's *Paranatural;* and MSNBC's *Countdown* with Keith Olbermann. Originally from the UK, Nick lives on the fringes of Dallas, Texas. He can be contacted at his blog: *http://NickRedfernFortean.blogspot.com.*